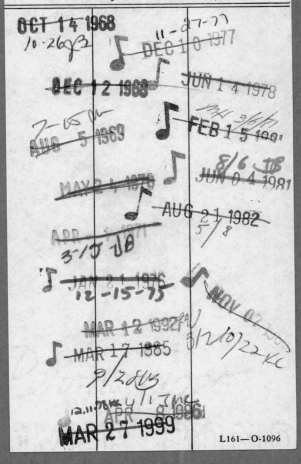

OPERA:

Grand and Not So Grand

By the same author:

THE MANY LIVES OF OTTO KAHN

OPERA STARS IN THE SUN

OPERA MANUAL

OPERA:
Grand
AND NOT SO
Grand

MARY JANE MATZ

WILLIAM MORROW & COMPANY, INC.

NEW YORK   1966

Chapt 1

No longer have to ask if opera
will survive — it will. Now
must ask where it succeeds
and where it failed & why?
Use this to predict where it
will go in future — who the
leaders will be & how they
will operate

Things To Do

1. ~~Talk to malcolm~~
2. ~~Go to placement office~~
3. ~~Go to music library~~
4. ~~Call Steve~~
5. Iron clothes
6. ~~Clean kitchen~~
7. ~~Read Math~~
8. Read Physics
9. Copy EE Notes
10. ~~Read EE~~
11. Start EE H.W.
12. ~~Run~~
13. ~~Wash hair~~
14. ~~Pick up shoes~~

CONTENTS

OPERA:

Grand and Not So Grand

CHAPTER

I

OPERA YESTERDAY
AND TODAY

Opera is a glorious spectacle, a splendid but uneven fabric of music, drama, dance, poetry, and stage architecture, imperfect by nature yet endowed with magic. It is also the child of an unstable marriage between art and business. When it first began to flourish, opera was pure and uncommercial, subsidized by royalty, nobility, and aristocracy; but after the first public opera house opened in Venice in 1637, opera became a marketable commodity, competing with popular entertainments, often sharing the stage with acrobats, ballets, magicians, and trained animals.

From that moment, opera was as much business as an art; its "artists" became "performers." In modern parlance, opera became a "property" to be handled, manipulated, and speculated upon. It remained in the hands of speculators for more than three hundred years; but now, at the mid-point of the twentieth century, the peak of the commercial era has been reached. Subsidy in one form or another is gradually reclaiming what it surrendered in the decades following 1637. One age is ending; another has already begun.

The future of opera seems secure. We no longer have to ask whether it will survive. But we may well ask where it succeeds and where it has failed, and why; and as the business of opera grows bigger, almost by the day, we want to predict a future

11

for it, and know who the masters of this empire will be, how they will operate, what will be their aims, their hopes, their motives.

Opera today confronts an hour of momentous change. Not even the building which houses it would be recognizable to past generations, for opera is leaving its old house—both physically and symbolically—and moving into new quarters. Until 1910 the opera house was a landmark in nearly every city and town in both Europe and the United States. Like the cathedral, the firehouse, and the city hall, the opera house was a fine, familiar monument, listed in guidebooks as one of the "sights to see." Many of these noble theaters have now been demolished. Many more have become movie or burlesque houses, supermarkets, garages, television studios, and office buildings. For in the last half-century, the face of the world has changed, and so has the face of opera.

Once, opera was easy to define, for it was serious and grand. Then the comic element was added, to be followed by the masque, operetta, and other cousins. Eventually opera came in all sizes, colors and degrees: *seria, semiseria, buffa,* grand, *comique, Kammer, Singspiel, lyrique,* light and intermezzo. Each of these types has its own shape, its own tone, although it takes an expert to tell one from another. All are performed today under the generic term "opera." But what is opera?

Anyone can recognize *Aida* and *La Gioconda* as opera. But opera is also *Amahl and the Night Visitors, La Périchole, Fledermaus, The Tale of a Soldier, The Ballad of Baby Doe, War and Peace, The Jumping Frog of Calaveras County, Hello Out There,* and *Night Flight,* though few operagoers of the eighteenth century would recognize them as such. And if these are opera, then what of *Porgy and Bess, My Darlin' Aida, Carmen Jones, The Most Happy Fella,* and *West Side Story?* If dialogue-heavy *Magic Flute* is opera, then these must also be opera. Perhaps Scarlatti would not recognize them, but he might not recognize the works of Giacomo Puccini or Richard Wagner or Lukas Foss either. Opera now is any drama couched chiefly in sung music. Beyond that, no definition is possible.

Since World War II, **opera has become unruly** and boisterous, pushing down the old walls which used to enclose it, extending its horizons and drawing an ever larger public, finding new houses and new interpreters. The man who swears he would never go to see *Aida* sits enthralled before his television screen to watch *Amahl*. He is not even aware that it is opera. The singer who dares not sing Otello or Norma feels comfortable in *Down in the Valley* and *Threepenny Opera*. Performances are still given in true opera theaters, but now also in university halls, conservatories, civic auditoriums, high schools and army camps, open air amphitheaters and gymnasiums, union halls and church basements, even at the high altar of Pittsburgh cathedral. Often it is more at home today in unglamorous surroundings than in the elegant confines of the opera house, for opera—no longer a pure and elevated art, no longer limited in intent—has penetrated every corner of the world, from Japan, China, Korea, and India down to the high-school stages in American small towns. What was once a cult has become commonplace, a major part of the explosive, vital theater and art renaissance of the 1950's and 1960's.

Everywhere abroad, new doors have been opened to opera by the national radio and television networks which both underwrite performances and transmit them. In the United States where the communications media have been less generous, the Maecenas of opera was originally the GI Bill of Rights, which pumped new blood into college, university, and conservatory opera departments. More recently, foundations have emerged as subsidizing agents, although to a very modest degree. The mania for phonographs and high-fidelity systems has added new recruits to the ranks of opera fans, while the inventors of wire recorders and magnetic tapes have also done their part, making it possible for the public to buy "an opera" at a local record shop and carry four hours of music around in one hand.

Having become fashionable among intellectuals, opera now attracts celebrated figures from the legitimate theater, from ballet, from the fine arts and films to serve as its directors, designers, and choreographers. Many of these high-paid "names" know nothing about opera and admit it. But opera is à la

mode; it is "in." Ingmar Bergman, Jean-Louis Barrault, Alfred
Lunt, and Laurence Olivier direct it. Salvador Dali and Jean
Cocteau and Marc Chagall design sets. Some literary figures
are actually working on librettos; others' works are being
adapted for opera or are already onstage. Even the Nobel Prize
poet Salvatore Quasimodo has tried his hand, becoming a librettist; and the names of Arthur Miller, Eugene O'Neill, Tennessee
Williams, Archibald MacLeish, William Saroyan, Luigi Piran-
dello, Berthold Brecht, Thornton Wilder, Stephen Vincent
Benet, Michel Butor, W. H. Auden, and Giuseppe di Lampe-
dusa have entered into the pavilion of opera through one door
or another.

Here, probably, lies a certain kind of salvation for opera: for
however these nonmusical (indeed, antimusical, in many cases)
figures may damage the traditional shapes of opera, at least they
draw attention to it and bring the paying public to the theater.
An opening night no longer draws a conclave of tiara-crowned
dowagers, decades out of fashion, or of titled aristocrats hung
with ancestral jewels. An opening night is what it must have
been three hundred years ago: a mixed bag of surprises, often
rowdy, completely democratic. Here, to be sure, pass couturier
gowns, rented jewels, and elegantly dressed young heads fresh
from Elizabeth Arden, Mr. Kenneth, or Alexandre. But here
too, mingling in the parade of grandeur, are students and "children of paradise," businessmen in gray suits, and women in
tailored attire or afternoon dresses. "Black tie is requested," says
the program of many European theaters, but it is no longer required. Opera again belongs to everyone, most especially in
Europe, from the president of a large corporation down through
the economic ranks to lathe operators from Milan factories. In
the audience are top-drawer aristocracy—families whose titles
reach back more than a thousand years—and members of the
international jet set; middle-class schoolteachers; and perhaps
the boy who sang *Amahl* in the Methodist church Christmas
production, if his parents can afford to take him. This is what
the democratization of the world has done for opera: returned
it to its seventeenth-century popularity. A part of the Metropolitan and La Scala public arrives by limousine, just as part of

the La Fenice public arrives in gondolas and motorboats. But another, very substantial part comes on foot and by subway, by chartered bus from schools or the outlying industrial suburbs. The evening opera audience walks by day in every way of life.

Signs of a boom are visible everywhere, though in America the boom is more apparent at the amateur than at the professional level. Big cities are engaged in building glittering, modern art-and-culture centers. Big opera companies are growing very rapidly. The smaller enterprises, with few exceptions, have never been so numerous; say nothing of the quality of their work, but give them credit simply for existing. Workshops have become a major factor in higher education as many colleges and universities now talk of engaging "artists in residence." Church groups, formerly content with badly costumed pageants, now stage opera regularly. So do high-school music departments. Countries such as Korea and India offer a new challenge to this theatrical art-form which once was cherished only in the rarefied air of Italian and Chinese court theaters.

Opera today is international rather than national. This is especially true on the top level (the Metropolitan, La Scala, Covent Garden, the Paris Opéra, Vienna's Staatsoper, Rome's Opera, Naples' San Carlo, the San Francisco Opera), but it is scarcely less true of smaller companies and repertory organizations. These in theory ought to have their own permanent roster of singers and never, or almost never, have a guest performer or let one of their own artists visit elsewhere. But even these tightly woven units occasionally succumb to the exchange fever which has swept the theater.

Singers today belong not to one city, but to the world. They and the famous directors and conductors and designers are shared by all the big theaters; opera is like a never-ending spring prom, with its invitations and programs signed up years in advance. To stay in one theater, even La Scala or the Metropolitan, is to be a wallflower.

The constant circulation of opera personnel lends a frightening homogeneity to the top-bracket performances. The world traveler who hears Leontyne Price in *Il Trovatore* in Milan or Joan Sutherland in *Lucia di Lammermoor* in London can be very sure of hearing the same artist in the same role in another operatic capital sooner or later. In the days of the stagecoach and relative immobility, only the artist circulated; the public stayed put. But now the public, too, travels, and these patterns of international exchange have created a new problem for the theater.

Singers no longer boast of having a repertory of two hundred operas which they sing in one or two or three cities. They have all become jet-age specialists, singing the same eight or ten operas in twenty or thirty different cities—over and over again, the same roles. And frequently these are the very roles which the singer has recorded once or twice, so that a pall of sameness falls over the whole industry, live or recorded.

Worse still, a small coterie of designers, conductors, and directors tour also. The Luchino Viscontis, the Franco Zeffirellis, the Teo Ottos, the Margherita Wallmanns, the Günther Rennerts all play the same international circuit as the singers. Visually, as well as aurally, this has led to an alarming standardization of the art. No one doubts that Visconti had something exciting and fresh to say about *La Traviata* when he first directed it at La Scala; no one doubts the originality of Zeffirelli's *La Bohème*. But when these directors have shown their style in a half-dozen big theaters, suddenly the smaller units begin to adopt their ideas or details. All the world begins to look the same.

This state of affairs has been aggravated even further by the current widespread custom of renting scenery (or even whole productions—singers, director, designer and all) from another city. See *Beatrice di Tenda* in Palermo, then move on to Venice and see the same opera with the same sets, which La Fenice has rented from Palermo. Dallas rents *Bohème* sets from Spoleto; Spoleto in its turn uses the Juilliard School of Music sets for *Il Conte Ory;* Lausanne rents the entire Spoleto production of *La Traviata,* even to Visconti's name on the posters. The Metropolitan rents *La Fanciulla del West* from Chicago. Philadelphia rents from New Orleans. Through the good offices of the invaluable Central Opera Service of the National Council of the Metropolitan, an impresario can find out which sets he can borrow (or rent) from which company, and perhaps even work out an exchange on even terms.

In these exchanges the question of snob appeal is obvious. The local impresario in Geneva, say, thinks that he boosts his prestige when he bills Visconti's *La Traviata* straight from the Spoleto Festival, with cast and sets complete. But he does not always do his city a service. As a matter of fact, Visconti's recent *Traviata* was not one of his best productions, nor was it one of Spoleto's best. (Far better was the *Salome,* which was leased intact by theaters in Trieste, Bologna, and other cities.) When the Geneva public is sitting watching "Visconti's" *Traviata,* Visconti is a thousand miles away, doing another production for another theater or sunning on the beach at Ischia. No matter. His name is on the posters outside, lending luster to a theater he may never have seen.

This may be a device to draw cultural snobs into the theater; but is it art? The production is old by the time it reaches Geneva, or any other city. The sets already begin to look shopworn. (And think of sets which have traveled across the Atlantic in the hold of a ship!) The cast has had its important rehearsals months before, in another theater, in another city. There is nothing fresh (and often very little which is exciting) about such a production. It would be far better for each city to use its own artists (or artists engaged for long enough periods to allow adequate rehearsal time with a director who will be there in the flesh and not merely in name) and its own sets, built for that theater and not doctored to make them fit the local stage. Because each city and each theater has a personality of its own, it is not always possible to adapt another theater's production successfully.

In some cases, but not all, it is cheaper to rent or lease another theater's production than to mount one. There is therefore a valid economic reason for using worn merchandise. Also the risk is slight, for if another theater has already put on the work, if the sets have already been used, then the impresario who is renting the production knows in advance what he is getting. He knows how Visconti's *La Traviata* looks and sounds, because he has seen it on Eurovision or in Spoleto. He knows that it is a success. He knows its weak points (in one European city, the original soprano was rejected by the renting company, and another substituted), knows also that it has been widely publicized; and there, too, he saves money and earns some. Saves, because he does not have to spend much to promote the production; earns, because people who have heard about it before come to the theater out of curiosity to see what Visconti's *Traviata* is like. For some perverse reason, audiences automatically believe that an imported production is better than one produced at home.

This is not always the case. Opera houses which are very proud of their productions eye with mistrust any theater which is "reduced" to importing casts and sets from other cities. German and East German and Eastern European theaters rarely borrow. They still think individually, not as part of a big international operation. But most of the professional theaters think alike; they think big. Big names, big productions, big budgets, big audiences, big publicity. As the size of urban centers has grown, so has the scale of opera. Of the fifteen largest cities in the world, all but three have big-scale opera as part of their regular cultural diet. Opera in the last fifteen years has become a one-world affair.

The protagonists of this book, then, are the people of this opera world—the composers, singers, conductors, stage directors and designers, press agents and claquers, the costumers, electricians and lighting experts, the scenery haulers, union agents, the public, and the critics. In short, all the men and women who paste this international collage together and make it a living, glowing art form.

This is the world of live—not dead—opera, a world of detail, exasperation, growth and, above all, workability, a complex machine which clacks away behind the diaphanous veils and tasseled curtains.

CHAPTER

II

THE SWOLLEN WORLD OF OPERA BUSINESS

"Il mondo dell'opera è il mondo dell'irrealtà." "The world of opera is the world of unreality," says Mario Labroca, the artistic director of the Teatro La Fenice in Venice. It is this very quality of fantasy which has made opera alluring for nearly four hundred years. But *irrealtà* is fast disappearing from the opera world. *Irrealtà* is giving way to IBM and Olivetti calculating machines, to printed contracts negotiated through unions and agents and managers, to committees in gray-flannel suits. Even the well-meaning clubwoman in the flowered hat, intent on "saving opera," is vanishing from the scene; that touch of magic, too, will go. Singers are social-security numbers. Music is played on tape through loud speakers as part of the opera's "score." Yesterday, it was the "world of unreality." Tomorrow, the world of cybernetics.

Even the repertory reflects these changes. Alessandro Scarlatti's *Il Mitridate Eupatore,* Gioacchino Rossini's *Il Turco in Italia,* Gaetano Donizetti's *Lucia,* Vincenzo Bellini's *La Sonnambula,* Giuseppe Verdi's *Aida,* Alfredo Catalani's *La Wally,* all are confined to the "world of unreality" by the fantasy of their settings and costumes. But *La Traviata, La Bohème,* and all subsequent operas of *verismo* coloring down to *Wozzeck, Lulù, The Consul,* and the Italian opera *Prize Fight* are slice-of-life reality. *Traviata* was read as realism even a century ago.

19

Thus we have a repertory with split personality. The dichotomy is evident even within the work of Menotti: *The Consul* is harshest reality, even though the dream scene distracts us briefly from this focus. *Amahl* and *The Last Savage,* on the other hand, belong to *"il mondo dell' irrealtà."*

Just as the repertory is split, so also the world of management, which is at the crossroads between the old-style impresario, who was a maverick, an individualist, and the new, huge industrial complex. In Verdi's time, and for two centuries before him, theaters were operated by a handful of people. Bartolomeo Merelli ran La Scala in the 1800's with a secretary (legman), a pair of office boys to carry mail, a small roster of singers, a small orchestra with one man (the conductor had not yet come into being) to put it through its paces, a small costume studio, and one or two scenery artists to draw the sketches and supervise the work of painting the sets. Today La Scala, like other big opera theaters, proudly points to the fact that a thousand people are employed there. Covent Garden's payroll numbered 851 in the season of 1961-62 and surpassed even that staggering figure to reach 897 in 1962-63 and 1,114 in 1964-65. The Metropolitan, with an annual budget of more than nine million dollars, employed a total of 1,314 in 1963-64 and will go far beyond that in its new house at Lincoln Center. (See chart, p. 21.)

The chiefs of these engorged empires are known by various titles: general manager, general administrator, *intendant, sovrintendente,* artistic director, sometimes president or chairman. Bolstered on all sides by assistants (assistant general administrator is one high-sounding title in general use, assistant-general-manager-in-charge-of is another) who are in turn hemmed in by secretaries, substrata assistants, office boys, switchboard operators, union officials, press agents, orchestra managers, backstage and out-front personnel, the director of a *modern opera corporation*—for this is what today's companies are—must also cope with his artists and boards of directors, chairman, fund raisers, attorneys, and (in the United States, at least) groups of well-intentioned, public-spirited women who stepped into the breach when it seemed that opera would die in the

1930's. If foundations and city government take over fund-raising chores, then the committee women can stay home. But the rest will remain, and their ranks will increase, according to the immutable, historic laws of bureaucracy.

Lest anyone think that these images of swollen anthills are an exaggeration, here are the official statements of three major theaters:

	Artists *	Orchestra	Stage and Staff	Adminis- tration and Out Front	Others	Total
Metropolitan, 1963-64	257	135	222	148	552	1,314
La Scala, 1963-64	370	140	240	70	180	1,000
Covent Garden, 1964-65	387	145	233	156	193	1,114

* Includes chorus and opera ballet, but not supers. The Metropolitan, for example, employs 400 supers, which are included in the final column ("Others"). La Scala does not include supers in its total figures. The Metropolitan total, withous supers, is 914. La Scala, with supers, employs 1,400 people.

This mass of numbers, multiplied by several hundred typewriters and computing machines, added to the subtotal of thousands of filing cabinets, tons of union cards and contracts in quadruplicate, telegrams and cables, social-security deductions and old-age-pensions and health-plan records, income-tax withholdings, complaints, charity benefits, and cigarette butts, makes up the composite picture of the modern opera house.

It is a complex world, too often more business than art.

First, there is the problem of raising money for the season or the year. Most artistic ventures do not pay their way with box-office receipts—opera least of all, because of the enormous cost of its productions. At the Metropolitan, where opera plays two hundred performances in New York and nearly fifty on tour (for a total of thirty-three weeks), the box office covers 74 per cent of the total costs. The highly profitable and shrewdly run Goldovsky Opera Theatre takes in 80 per cent of its expenses at the box office; but an experimental and daring enterprise such as the Santa Fe Opera realizes only 33 per cent of its expenses from the paying public. Some large European theaters cover only 30 per cent of expenses with box-office receipts; La Scala, less than 20 per cent.

To add to the box-office take, opera companies sell their performances and their names to broadcasting and recording companies. The Metropolitan regularly rents its house—and has since the company was founded—to ballet and theater companies after the opera season closes.

But all these commercial efforts combined cannot close the gap between income and expenditure. In the early centuries of opera the theater operated gambling casinos in the large salon rooms of the house: this, of course, is the *ridotto*, which took its name from the small (or "reduced") orchestra which played there to entertain its patrons. But in America and many European countries, legalized gambling has been limited to certain areas—Las Vegas, for example—while in some cities, such as Venice, the *ridotto* or casino is run for the benefit of the city itself, not the opera house. Restaurants, and social rooms, too, provide a small source of income. But there still remain each year enormous sums to be raised.

In Europe and South America, government subsidy is the answer. In 1965, Italy gave $12,800,000 in subsidy to opera houses (in thirteen cities) of the national theater chain. These include La Scala, the San Carlo in Naples, La Fenice in Venice, the Comunale in Florence, the Massimo Bellini in Catania, the Massimo in Palermo, the Opera in Rome, the Verdi in Trieste, and five other theaters in cities such as Parma, Turin, and Genoa. Other countries are more (or less) generous; but state subsidy is a rule abroad.

America is not so fortunate. Our opera companies must go, hat in hand, to individuals, corporations, foundations, community funds. All the humiliating and debilitating mechanics of fund-raising lie behind each dollar spent. In the past, the individual patron bore the burden of responsibility. But as the recent Rockefeller Brothers' Fund "Report on the Performing Arts" proves, this fountain is running dry. Donations have become more numerous, but they have become smaller. The era of Otto Kahn and Louis Eckstein is past. Only rarely, only in art-conscious communities, does heavy support from individual pa-

trons save the season. At the Metropolitan, for example, under-
writing the deficit is a matter of personal choice: subscribers are
"invited" to pay 20 per cent more for their tickets than they are
required to do. The San Francisco Opera assesses some of its
boxholders regularly. Chicago uses a guarantor system, as did
many companies of the decades between 1900-1929. And many
opera-giving organizations use "guilds," which are supporting
organizations, to shape local taste and awaken civic conscience.
The Metropolitan Opera Guild, for example, adds its contribution to the National Council of the Met; the total gift of both
organizations in 1963-64 was $360,000. The remainder of the
deficit was made up by contributions from subscribers and individual opera enthusiasts. But Rudolf Bing, the Metropolitan's
general manager, is constantly looking for new sources of support. He believes—and it is a conviction shared by most managers in the United States—that most individuals are now giving
as much as they can reasonably be expected to give.

The sole exceptions to this, curiously, seem to be the securer
income groups earning between $5,000 and $10,000 per annum.
These groups, according to the Rockefeller report, give less than
the poor or the rich, proving that the artist's traditional mistrust
of the middle class is quite sound. The most astonishing and dis-
maying single fact unearthed by the Rockefeller Brothers' panel
is that people in the lower-income brackets contribute more of
their incomes than the people in the $5,000-$100,000 brackets.
An Italian proverb counsels, "When you are desperate, look to
the poor man, not to the rich." And in this matter of contributions, the old peasant wisdom seems to have reached the core
of the problem. Internal Revenue tables prove that people with
adjusted gross incomes of less than $2,500 give 5.8 per cent of
their incomes for charitable purposes, while people in the
$10,000 to $15,000 bracket give only 3.0 per cent; people in the
bracket from $50,000 to $100,000 only 4.3 per cent. It is not
until the $100,000 to $150,000 bracket is reached that giving
matches the generosity of the nearly destitute.

Foundations, apparently, do much less than the public commonly thinks. In the words of the Rockefeller Brothers' report,
"foundations, large and small, national and local, could play a

significantly larger role in the development of the arts then they have in the past." Perhaps because foundations give first to educational and scientific enterprises, perhaps because they regard the disorderly world of the theater as unworthy of their support, perhaps because a deep vein of philistinism and mistrust of creative people lies beneath the smooth foundation façade, foundations have not yet helped opera significantly. The Ford Foundation grants, discussed later in this chapter, may represent a significant breakthrough.

Opera needs money. And wherever money is lacking, opera fails. This elemental truth lies behind the collapse of dozens of professional companies all over America. School workshops flourish because they are subsidized.

After the problems of fund raising come problems of scheduling. Today, as in past centuries, all theaters are run according to one of two standard systems: the repertory system and the *stagione* system. The first represents the traditional northern, German system of operation; the second is the Italian or southern method.

Under the *stagione* system, the opera year is divided into several "seasons" of four, six, or ten weeks each. The most important of these has always been the fashionable and exciting winter season, called *Carnevale-Quaresima* or Carnival and Lent. Technically this begins on the day after Christmas and ends at Easter, though opera companies have pushed this opening date back as far as possible, sometimes into early December, sometimes into November. The second season or *stagione* is *Primavera,* spring, which runs from the Monday after Easter until the last day of June. The summer season, rare in very hot countries unless the performances are part of a festival, runs through July, August, and September. During the summer, theaters are dependent largely on tourists for support. *Autunno* or autumn is the last season of the year, beginning in October and ending in early December. In all Italian theaters, or theaters under Italian influence, the *Carnevale-Quaresima* means the best audience, the most attention, the highest fees, the greatest prestige.

Sometimes the general manager fixes the dates of his seasons;

sometimes he works it out with the local tourist agencies or chambers of commerce. In Genoa in 1825, for example, it was the Senate itself which legislated the opening and closing dates of the *stagioni*. In other cities it was a matter between local governments (or police) and the impresario. Today, some cities have opera in all of these seasons—Venice, which leans heavily on tourist and entertainment revenue, is a case in point—but others have opera only during Carnival and Lent. Milan calls a halt in June, but Rome moves out to the Baths of Caracalla. Chicago's Lyric Opera performs only in the autumn, but San Francisco, which used to have opera only in September and October, now has added a spring season.

Companies using the *stagione* system base their operation on the Italian method of opera production. They put on a given number of works ranging from three or four (in a city such as Treviso, Italy, or Houston, Texas) to twenty (in Milan). For each of these operas a separate cast of singers is assembled for the lead roles and a separate conductor is hired. The artists arrive at the theater shortly before the *prima:* sometimes a week or two in advance, sometimes only a day or two before. They rehearse with the orchestra and stage crew, preparing for the *anteprova* (a pre-dress-rehearsal) and the *prova generale* (a dress rehearsal which, in Italy and other Latin countries and sometimes in England and America, is attended by the critics who write their reviews based on what they hear that night). With only this much preparation (sometimes enough, sometimes not enough), the company goes onstage and performs on the night of the *prima* and for three or four or five successive performances after it.

The management of a company which uses the *Stagione* system may then abandon this production altogether, as most of the American civic companies must in order to keep public interest alive, or may hope that it can assemble the same cast and conductor for the same work next year. The perfect example of the revived *stagione* success was the Callas-Visconti *Traviata* at La Scala, which played twenty-one performances in two seasons to sold-out houses and thus set some kind of record for *stagione* opera in the postwar era. In Verdi's day, manage-

ment staged fewer works with longer runs (from ten to seven-
teen or twenty, or even more, consecutive performances if the
opera were a success), but the system was basically the same.
When the public tires of a particular opera, or when an important singer from the cast has to go on to another engagement, then another work is scheduled. It, in turn, runs its three
or more performances and then is withdrawn.

The *stagione* system is as old as opera itself. It is based on
the talents of visiting firemen, who are hired for one specific
season or one specific opera. It is common not only in Italy, but
also in Monaco, Turkey, Egypt, Spain, Portugal, Mexico, Japan,
all of South America, and in many American cities such as San
Francisco, Chicago, Tulsa, and Miami. Everywhere, the leading
singers, most of the secondary singers, and some or all of the
chorus are imported from other cities or countries via the good
offices of an operatic theatrical agent, whose entire living may
be realized from the percentage he takes. This can range from
10 per cent to 50 per cent or even 100 per cent (depending on
how honest he is, how strong the artist is, and how many government regulations hem him in) of the fees of the singers
whom he farms out for the *stagione* performances. Ten per cent
is considered a regular agent's fee. Anything over 25 per cent is
unfair, though many European agents take more than that.
When more than half of the salary is given back by the artist to
the impresario or manager of the theater, the singer is victim
of a "kickback." One of the chief functions of musicians' unions
is to prevent kickbacks.

The shortcomings of the *stagione* system are obvious. The
company is often ill-prepared and the musical execution may
be slapdash, if one or more artists arrive at the last minute. (In
the case of the Italian première of Menotti's *Last Savage* at
Venice, for example, the leading soprano engaged for the role
of Kitty came when the rehearsals were already well along and
the opening night was only two weeks away. At that late date,
she announced that she didn't know any of the music. She was
removed from the cast and the stand-in was given the part.) It
takes a very strong conductor to shape up a production of a
difficult work in ten days or two weeks. On the other hand, the
theater management which uses the *stagione* system can, if it

is lucky, get exactly the voices it wants for a given opera, and with sufficient money, it can sign four or five of the best voices of the day. When an internationally famous conductor is added, he—using the force of his own genius—can often make even the most modest theater's orchestra sound good. When the cards fall right, the result is pure operatic gold. A good example in the United States is Carol Fox's Chicago Lyric Opera, which has put together some of the best performances of the postwar era on the *stagione* system. But the whole history of opera is studded with examples of superb *stagione* performances, from the days of Vittoria Archilei down to the present.

At the opposite pole of opera production is the repertory system, which is almost universally used in Germany, Austria, Belgium, Holland, the Scandinavian countries, Russia, and the countries of Eastern Europe. It is also used to some extent in the Paris Opéra and Comique, which grew from the Royal Academy of France (1671), said to be the first permanent opera-producing organization in the world. The repertory is also used at the Metropolitan, as far as possible. Arturo Toscanini, when he held the reins at La Scala (1921-29) managed to convert even that incorrigible *stagione* house to repertory. As Harold Rosenthal pointed out in *Opera* Magazine, July, 1963, it was possible to see six different operas in a week or ten days in Milan in the 1920's, just as it is possible to see a great variety of works in New York or in any German city today during a limited period. In cities where the *stagione* system is used, the public's choice may be limited to one or two operas per week.

In the first centuries of opera, the singers engaged for a given *stagione* were only a dozen or so, plus a small chorus. A famous soprano—Giuseppina Strepponi, who much later became Verdi's wife, is a good example—would be engaged to sing three or four operas (all of the operas on the *cartellone* of the season) at a given theater. Here is Strepponi's schedule for Teatro La Fenice in Venice for 1836:

April 9	*La Gazza Ladra*
April 23	*I Puritani*
May 4	*La Cenerentola*
May 7	*Nina Pazza per Amore*

Because all the operas were written within a given stylistic frame and sung in one language, each company could have one prima donna or, at great risk, two (trouble sometimes resulted when two were hired), and one or two supporting female voices, a pair of high male voices (sometimes a *primo tenore* or *musico*), two or three low male voices, and a chorus. In short, a small and manageable ensemble.

In the heyday of Italian opera, the total personnel—onstage, backstage, and "upstairs"—was forty for a small theater, sixty or seventy for a more important house. Compare this with the 1,314 on record for the Met in 1963-64, and the giantism of twentieth-century opera becomes apparent at once.

The immense complexity of the operation is only hinted at in the following glance at a Metropolitan season, described by Robert Herman for *Opera News:*

"An opera season is like a jigsaw puzzle, and it takes nearly *two years* of planning to put together . . . Not for one minute during our twelve-hour day are we permitted to forget that we must try to please some 700 employees (133 of them singers), over 700,000 operagoers, millions of radio listeners and at least a dozen music critics. We are also responsible to those who make up our deficits, which now amount to well over a million dollars a year, and to others who give us new productions to the tune of, say, $135,000 (for this season's new *Aida*)." The Metropolitan's seats, however, cost only slightly more than they did in the early 1900's.

The big opera company functions like a large industrial corporation. It deals with unions, boards of directors, lending organizations, entrepreneurs, shipping companies, travel agencies, itineraries, hotel reservations, truckers, train schedules. Budgets, like deficits, run to astronomical figures, such as those cited in the paragraph above. All this bigness inevitably has an effect on the productions. All sense of intimacy is lost. To get some idea of how opera has outgrown its britches, merely consider that it is not uncommon to see as many as fifty people *backstage,* even in small theaters, in addition to those singing for the audience. A theater such as the Verdi in Trieste or the La Fenice in Venice now employs an average of sixty-five singers, about ten conductors, plus orchestra, chorus, and ballet, during a given season. For every one of these, there are two or three *unseen* employees somewhere else in the house. *Yet the size of the theater itself and the number of seats in the house are the same as when the total ensemble numbered sixty.*

Nearly every opera company is constantly preoccupied with problems of deficit and of balancing the budget. Yet no one seems to have considered trimming some of this excess backstage fat from the productions, for we are not only in an era of bigness, we are also in an era of Production rather than Music.

This is the epoch of the stage director and of closed-circuit intramural television. How bloated it all is! We are far from the day when the management's chief concern was the engagement of a star soprano; far from the day when the impresario sat down at his desk, drew a sheet of writing paper from the drawer, and wrote longhand to Maria Malibran to ask her to lend her luster to his season; farther still from the day when Malibran, receiving his letter, sat before her writing table and wrote:

> "Let it be an *opera seria,* or let it be something else which my charming colleague Rossini will choose. I will not refuse then to play these taxing roles three nights a week, if this will help the theater administration . . . Adieu, and a thousand good wishes,
> Malibran."

Malibran is dead. So also is her spirit of generosity and the sense of *club intime* which used to suffuse all theaters, large and small. The opera house has become a corporate monster in which there is too little rapport between artists and management. Only in the repertory theaters is there any sense of loyalty; outside them, it is dog-eat-dog. Artists protest constantly against the coldness of management, while management, on its side, complains that the singers are bandits, ruining their budgets by holding out for exorbitant fees.

Nearly one hundred years ago, and in a different context, Verdi admonished one of his contemporaries:

"Let's go back to old times: it will be a step forward."

Torniamo all'antico: sarà un progresso. It is a point which might be well taken by opera theaters today.

But it may be too late. Intimacy and delicacy may never again play a role in the theater. Perhaps the bursting forth of the theater renaissance *at a time when bigness is the criterion of quality* has ruled out any future return to the old intramural comradeship. The cultural boom, the cultural explosion, has put opera and all other art into the big money. According to *The New York Times,* Americans spent nearly $400,000,000 in 1964 in theaters, opera houses, and concert halls. The present trend toward huge civic arts-centers (such as Lincoln Center in New York, the cultural center in Los Angeles, the new Arts Center in Detroit) will eventually provide this growing industry with a massive architectural frame: centralized, highly organized, impersonal. To "megalopolis" and "multiversity" will be added "monstropera," as barren of beauty and human values as a many-leveled, automated parking garage.

CHAPTER

III

THE DESPERATE IMPRESARIOS

Renaissance, baroque, or modern, the opera impresario or manager has rarely had an easy life. Not since opera divorced itself from courts and aristocratic houses has the manager been comfortable; he is traditionally nervous, excitable, disorganized, harried. This image, at least, has changed little since 1637.

One of the apocryphal legends of opera concerns the nineteenth-century Bolognese impresario Francesco Mionei. When he was handed the financial statement of his season, Mionei glanced at the column where the deficit figure was written and dropped to the floor with heart failure. His first underwriter was called in. He, too, looked at the statement and died. A second underwriter, Signor Mazzini, was made of stronger stuff. He survived the blow and, presumably, somehow discharged the debt.

Today the risks in opera management are not so great, the mortality rate not so high—though all theater managers would deny this. The picture began to change, in fact, shortly after the death of Mionei, in Bologna itself, where for the first time the municipal government offered the opera house rent-free to anyone with courage enough to try to put on an opera season. A municipal fund was also made available to the opera company. The modern opera business structure dates from this time.

From 1637 until recently, the opera impresario occupied an

equivocal and not always enviable position. First, he had to find a theater and rent it for a season. Second, he had to get together enough singers to make an opera company. Third, he had to choose the repertory, with at least one eye cocked toward the public from whose pockets came the money which would make his fortune or—more frequently—let him break even. Last, he had to find underwriters who would lend him enough to cover his enterprise until the box-office returns began to match the evening's expenses.

The impresario—today, in musical comedy and legitimate theater and movie circles, he is called "the producer"—was frequently a conniving opportunist. The records of his business deals through the history of opera leave little doubt about his character: singers unpaid, companies stranded, backers deceived, mistresses given choicest roles. He was unschooled and often coarse: illiterates actually became impresarios of fairly stable opera companies. Thus he was the butt of jokes from all sides.

"The *modern* impresario must not have any understanding whatsoever of the theater business, nor of music, librettos, scenic design, etc. . . . ." writes Benedetto Marcello with fine irony in his *Il Teatro alla Moda*, published in the early 1700's. "When he gets the libretto from the librettist, he will go straight to the Prima Donna, even before he reads it, and beg her to hear it through; when it is read, the Prima Donna will be there, and also her Lover, her Lawyer, the Prompters, a couple of Porters, some of the Supers, the Wardrobe Master, the Music Copyist, the Comedian, the Lover's Valet, etc.; and each of them will give his opinion of the libretto, now this is bad, and that won't do. And the Impresario will answer them all smoothly saying 'Everything will be taken care of.'

"He will hand over the opera to the Director on the fourth of the month, saying that it has to get onstage by the twelfth, and don't pay any attention to the music because we have to get through this quickly . . .

"He will hand over the part of the Son to a Male Lead who is at least twenty years older than the Stage Mother . . . When the Big Shots in the cast complain about their parts, the Impresario gives an *express order* to the Librettist and the Composer to tear up the whole opera in order to satisfy them.

"He gives away free tickets every night to the Doctor, the Lawyer, the Druggist, the Barber, the Carpenter, his Godfather and all his Friends and to all their families, to guarantee that the house is never empty; and just to make sure, he asks all the leading singers, the conductor, the orchestra members, the supers to bring five or six people each to the theatre on free tickets.

"He sees to it that Women make up the greater part of the Company; and if two Prima Donnas fight over who is to have the leading role, then the Impresario makes the Librettist write two roles which are absolutely equal in the number of Arias, Verses and Recitatives, making sure that even the names of the two characters have exactly the same *number of syllables*.

"At the end of the Performance, he will knock off a little bit here and there from the salaries of the Double Bass and 'Cello players, claiming that they didn't play certain parts of the score, and he will beg the Composer to score the opera without Double Bass and 'Cello, as far as it is possible to do so. Then he will cheat the Leading Singers, saying that they had colds, that they were off key, etc., and thus he pares down their fees.

"He will hire cheap Male Leads, and Women whose careers are finished, being sure that they have lots of rich Protectors, but not that they are Stars . . . And he will pay Round Trip Tickets to the foreign Stars to be sure that they come, promising them a good Hotel near the Theatre, Food, Linens, etc., and then he will lodge them in some *little closet* (near the Theatre, of course) . . .

"When the Theatre is half-empty, the modern Impresario will let his Stars sing just half of their Arias, let the Recitatives go, let people laugh out loud in their boxes, etc. . . .

"And he will take his Married Prima Donnas, when they are pregnant and put them on the stage as a Pregnant Queen or Pregnant Empress . . ."

"*Basta!*" as Benedetto Marcello himself would exclaim in his exasperation at the ludicrous state of things. Yet the truth about operatic impresarios is even wilder than *Il Teatro alla Moda* would have it.

The impresario got his foothold in the theater just as opera itself began to change from a solemn court entertainment to a free-for-all open to anyone who had the money to pay for a seat. At the very start, that is to say in the years between 1637 and 1670, the opera companies had no impresario. The singers themselves got together enough funds to keep their companies going; and their "manager," if indeed he can be given such a high-sounding title, was the Male Comic Lead.

When the Venetian patrician family Tron, the owners of the Teatro San Cassiano, which was the first opera house in the world, leased the theater to Manelli and Ferrari and their Roman opera company, there was no precedent to follow in the business arrangements. The Trons reserved all the boxes for themselves; these they either gave or sold to their friends or else put up for public sale. The company had the right to sell only the orchestra seats, which were lower on the social scale than anything else in the theater—even the Italian name *platea,* which survives to this day, suggests how base they were. This was the Elizabethan pit, and it was an inferno indeed. The "angels" in the *loggione*—the gallery up near the roof—were better off than the public in the *platea;* for though the *loggione* was smelly, at least one would not be bombarded during the performance with whatever fell down from above: leaflets, the remains of suppers eaten in the boxes, sometimes overripe fruit and vegetables destined for a hapless singer, or occasionally a chair which an angry paying customer aimed at the stage.

The Tron family, and other early patricians, kept the best seats for themselves, for in these early years the company was in no position to bargain. But all this changed rapidly. The vogue of opera became a mania. From having one opera theater in 1637 (the San Cassiano), Venice alone leaped forward until by 1699 there were sixteen opera houses in the city. The fever spread to Bologna, Rome, Naples, Florence. Overnight, almost, opera became a big business.

Sometimes the impresario rented the theater for one season of five or six weeks only. Sometimes (as in the case of the San

Cassiano in Venice) the theater was leased for as long as ten years at a time. The impresario's contract stipulated that he lease the "stage, curtains, the stage machinery, the ropes, drops, costumes, and all the other equipment having to do with the performances of opera." But the owner of the theater (in this case, the Tron family) held everything else. Often the proprietors managed, one way or another, to pocket the box-office receipts as well. The impresario's lot was not always a happy one.

However, he could console himself with what he extorted from prima donnas and their protectors, from composers whom he sometimes charged to put their works onstage. He got the receipts from the sale of librettos, the sale of seats in the *platea* and *loggione,* the sale of candles used to read librettos in the dark, and the sale of sweets and ice cream sold by vendors who circulated through the audience during the performance itself, like modern, burlesque-house candy butchers. (In Chinese opera houses these sweets vendors still disturb the performance. In the West they are now confined to the bar or lobby, their sales limited to intermissions.) In addition, the impresario frequently took the profits from the gambling casino which was in the theater. Often the income from the gambling rooms exceeded that earned from the performances themselves.

The impresario was an "operator" in the worst sense of that word. He cut his expenses wherever he could—and in many more areas than Benedetto Marcello indicates. He hired fewer orchestra players than necessary, failed to provide sufficient illumination (so that howls of anger and shouts of "Light! Light!" frequently punctuated the performances), used cheap costume fabrics, cut down the number of extras in the crowd scenes.

Abuses were frequent; and the paying public quickly learned that its only recourse was to raise enough uproar during a bad performance to guarantee the next opera's being better. Hubbub and protest became a commonplace in opera theaters; and the title "impresario" came to be a synonym for scurrilous dealings. Soon the owners of the theaters had to write contracts which guaranteed that "the dignity of the theater be maintained," and that a certain number of operas be put on with a certain rank of singers. Occasionally the owner even specified the names of the singers to be hired, so that cheating on the vocal level, at least, might be reduced to a minimum. But the impresario continued by tradition, to cheat. He was a cross between businessman, speculator, artistic director, usurer and whoremonger. One Piemontese was also a marriage broker who engaged unmarried prima donnas and sold them to gentlemen in the various cities where his troupe performed.

Impresarios were for the most part ignorant of music, but they did not hesitate to impose their will upon even the most famous composers, cutting and rearranging librettos and scores haphazardly to guarantee success with the public and a big box-office return. They encouraged the outrageous tyranny of the singer, who was the darling of the public. In short, they abused their position so regularly and flagrantly that theater owners were forced to appoint policing committees to keep the impresarios in line.

It is not until the 1800's that the modern theatrical businessman began to emerge; and even he is tainted with the soiled reputation of his predecessors. This was the epoch of the great Italian "managers" of the nineteenth century: Domenico Barbaja, the "discoverer" of Rossini, Bellini, and Donizetti, impresario of the San Carlo in Naples and of Viennese theaters as well; Alessandro Lanari of Florence, the Sol Hurok of his day; Bartolomeo Merelli of La Scala in Milan, the man who gave Verdi his first chance to be heard onstage.

We have Stendhal to thank for the following sketch of Barbaja: "sometime waiter in a coffee house, who by gambling, and more especially by holding the bank at faro and by running a gaming house, had amassed a fortune worth several millions. . . . He was among the host of French army-contractors who were making and losing fortunes every six months in the wake of the battalions . . . He realized at once, from the way in which Rossini's musical reputation was spreading abroad in society, that here was a young composer who might be good or bad, but who, rightly or wrongly, was going to be the coming figure in the world of music . . . Rossini, who was used to dealing with the seediest of fourth-rate *impresarî* in a perpetual state of flagrant bankruptcy, was astonished to find himself sought out by a millionaire who in all probability would count it beneath his dignity to embezzle twenty *sequins* out of his salary."

Merelli began in the theater as the librettist of Johann Simon Mayr, Nicola Vaccai, and Gaetano Donizetti, then went on to become a theatrical agent. "Between ourselves, he passes for a swindler," wrote Bellini in a letter. Bellini later accused Merelli of peddling pirated scores of his music. Donizetti complained that Merelli made unauthorized changes in his scores and accused him of hiring a tenor for a given part and then making him play cello in the company orchestra. "He ruins operas, he ruins voices; the public hears mutilated versions of every part . . . The Italian season here in Vienna was Hell let loose . . . What howls! What cat-calls! What a lesson for the good Merelli!"

Merelli, reputed to be an Austrian spy during the Italian *Risorgimento,* was nevertheless the discoverer of Verdi, and the impresario who staged *Oberto, Conte di San Bonifacio,* Verdi's first opera. When the second work, *Un Giorno di Regno* proved to be a total fiasco, Merelli still kept faith with Verdi, kept encouraging him to compose yet one more opera, and finally forced upon the composer the libretto of *Nabucco,* the work which was to make Verdi famous. Merelli ruled La Scala from 1836 to 1863, with the exception of some seasons between 1850 and 1861. Yet even Verdi, who had every reason to be grateful to him, broke with him in the 1840's and specifically stated in each of his opera contracts that the première *not* be given at La Scala. Impresarios were, even at this late date, under a cloud of mistrust and suspicion.

It was not until around 1850 that Frederick and Ernest Gye in London, and Benjamin Lumley, James Mapleson and Max Maretzek in America began to lend the odor of respectability to the trade of impresario. These men and their successors, Giulio Gatti-Casazza, Edward Johnson, and Gaetano Merola of San Francisco, knew the theater, and were honest with their artists and with the public. But they soon were forced to give up their one-man rule. Operas in the twentieth century are spectacles on a grand scale, given with singers whom it is impossible to cheat, with elegant costumes designed by top-name theatrical wardrobe studios, with big orchestras, and with choruses running to fifty or seventy-five singers (instead of the twelve who used to serve). Just as in the Middle Ages it was possible for one noble to build an entire monastery at his personal expense, so it was once possible for a single man to put on opera. This is no longer the case; today no single man can put together these opera extravaganzas. In America, as in Europe, the funds for a given company come from many pockets—private or state—and the old-time impresario has given way to committees of businessmen or guilds of socially prominent women who consider it their duty to raise funds for "culture."

The last of the nineteenth-century breed in the United States (there are still several impresarios at work in Latin countries) is Alfredo Salmaggi, born in Aquila in the Abruzzi, long-time resident of Brooklyn. Salmaggi is a one-man enterprise, Barnum and Belasco in one, a veritable conjurer when money matters are in hand. At the poker and *scopa* tables he has Caruso's killer instinct, which for five decades he has carried over into his theatrical business dealings. Salmaggi can cook, intimidate gangsters, singers, and union officials; hoodwink the public and keep it entertained; chastise his nine sons and daughters (several of whom are in the opera business in their own right); edit and publish a magazine after writing all the copy himself. He also finds time to put on opera: his record is a nearly unbelievable total of five thousand performances in forty-three years. Salmaggi entrusts the details of casting, staging, and publicizing to no one. Under duress, he even appears onstage in costume, sometimes to save a twenty-dollar fee which he would otherwise have to pay to a small-parts singer, sometimes to replace one of his cast who has fallen drunk in the wings.

Salmaggi's henna hair, his trademark in show business, hangs wavy and abundant, just short of his shoulders. It frames a wide, fierce, handsome face which has the unlikely bone structure of an American Indian. He wears a white flannel suit, cut in the fashion of the thirties. From time to time he snaps the brim of a spanking-white fedora which sweeps across his shoulders.

Salmaggi has put on opera for nearly fifty years in South and Central America, in the Caribbean and Italy, and all over Canada and the United States; but his home base has been the Brooklyn Academy of Music, where his Popular Price Grand Opera Company was installed.

On the nights when he has performances, Salmaggi greets the public in the foyer of the theater, distributing the largesse of his big, coarse handshake and wishing everyone a "good time inside."

To his friends Salmaggi confides that he is not always in the lobby just to welcome the public. On nights when the money at hand fails to cover the musicians' fees, he says, he waits at the box office to harvest the receipts, then rushes backstage to pay the singers so that the performance may begin. Asked if this state of affairs prevails often, Salmaggi answers, "Most every night"; yet he has remained solvent for a very long time, as operatic careers are reckoned.

When Salmaggi determined to found an opera company as a showcase for his pupils, he chose *Pagliacci* as the inaugural opera and announced that he would sing the leading role himself. Salmaggi rented the Brooklyn Academy for one night, but his success was such that he and his sons are still entrenched there, nearly fifty years later.

Salmaggi quickly gathered to himself the same noisy audience which remains loyal today. He encourages the kind of behavior which has always been frowned upon at the Met and other dignified theaters: if the public whistles, howls, jeers, or roars with enthusiasm, if it throws the scraps from box lunches down from the balcony, Salmaggi smiles and rubs his big hands together. He cannot bear coldness in an audience. Better to be booed than to be received politely. He regales his public with little curtain speeches about his home life and tantalizes them with announcements of treats in store: "Next week, right here at the Academy, *Il Trovatore* with Giovanni Martinelli—" murmurs of astonishment from the audience "—in box number five!"—A roar of laughter and jeers.

Encores have always been one of the special appeals of Salmaggi's companies—also of the now defunct San Carlo and
Philadelphia La Scala and other companies of the same ilk. The
Metropolitan has enforced a house rule against encores since
the night the Russian bass Feodor Chaliapin stepped out of
character (King Philip II of Spain) in *Don Carlo* to stride out
to the footlights and shout across the orchestra to order the
conductor to begin again for his encore of *"Ella giammai
m'amò."* But Salmaggi has never been so strict. He equates
encores with money in the bank. His public loves him for his
generosity. But they love him even when he gulls them and
admits it. Such is the intimate nature of the relationship of the
old-time impresario and his audience.

In the 1920's and 1930's, when union restrictions on performances were few, Salmaggi recalls that he would gather his company together in New York and let each member pay his own
way: to Rochester, Cleveland, or even Havana. If the performances drew, they shared the profits. If not, no one had lost more
than his fare and his energy. There were no guarantees, no
advances, and sometimes no fees. But everyone took an optimis-
tic and characteristically Italian view of this precarious life,
trouping joyfully, sharing hotels and dressing rooms, playing
poker in train coaches through the night, and eating big plates
of macaroni in inexpensive Italian restaurants. "We got twelve
portions of macaroni, twelve meats, four bottles of wine, coffee
—and the bill was four dollars. Sometimes we didn't even pay.
Che bei tempi! What beautiful times!" Salmaggi mourns that
long-dead spirit of camaraderie which has almost vanished in
the big-business atmosphere pervading opera today.

When Salmaggi could save money by taking over a role himself, he hurried into costume. He has played Harlequin in
Pagliacci, the major-domo in *Traviata* and Parpignol in *Bohème*.
These little savings mount up. Not even a major role daunts
him. In one of his rare encounters with German opera, he
found himself at curtain time without a Venus for *Tannhäuser*
at the New York Hippodrome, formerly the Manhattan center
for Salmaggi's activities. Reassuring his skeptical cast, Salmaggi
snatched a shirred mauve-chiffon gown from the wardrobe, ar-

ranged a blond wig over his long henna hair, and flung himself onto Venus' couch in a seductive pose. The orchestra, tenor, and conductor scarcely got through the Venusberg scene; the chorus and other principals spilled over from the wings, where they had gathered to watch. It is an index to the *italianità* of Salmaggi's audience that *no one realized that anything was amiss*, though Salmaggi only pantomimed the action while the convulsed orchestra improvised Venus' vocal line.

The smallest audience Salmaggi ever drew numbered 149, for a *Fedora*. But Salmaggi says he lost nothing because the soprano had paid for the whole production. Salmaggi admits that he has at least once accepted money from singers; but he philosophizes that if anyone is fool enough to pay to sing, he deserves to be fleeced. *"Il vero impresario non paga nessuno,"* Salmaggi declares. "The true impresario never pays anybody." This is the last faint echo of the traditional opera theater.

His tactics have earned Salmaggi much criticism from self-appointed protectors of operatic dignity. His time-worn scenery and stylized stage techniques make opera ridiculous, they say. Costumes dating from the twenties and thirties destroy illusion. His singers are sometimes old, sometimes inexperienced, sometimes not even sober. But one charge which has never been leveled at him is dullness.

Salmaggi and those few who linger on from his epoch lift opera joyfully from the trough of "respectability" and illuminate it with life and humor. They puncture the balloon of pomposity and bring art down to earth. They perform theater music in the theater, never forgetting that the first function of opera is to entertain.

In the music business, people sometimes say that Salmaggi will do anything for money. This is not true. He is an impresario in the old, grand style—emotional, sentimental, lovable, garrulous, warm. Salmaggi, like his Italian predecessors, cannot surrender his illusions, for they are the foundation stones of his world. A fitting tribute was recently paid Salmaggi when, in 1966, the Italian government decorated him for his lifetime of service to opera.

Salmaggi is unique in the contemporary world of opera,

though some of the impresarios of the 1920's and 1930's shared his love for opera, if not his approach to it. One of the most feared and revered of the older generation was Gaetano Merola, the founder of the San Francisco Opera, which in the United States ranks next in prestige to the Metropolitan.

Merola had a magic touch with opera. Elegant in his soft gray vests and fine handmade shirts, slender, immensely sophisticated and self-confident, Merola possessed an unfailing instinct about opera. He knew voices—no one better than he—and was on first-name terms with everybody in the world—even the Pope, according to a long-standing joke in the opera world. Merola could cast a spell over singers to get the best out of them. Some of the performances of Merola's first years at San Francisco are legends now: *Mefistofele* with Beniamino Gigli, Adam Didur, and Bianca Saroya in 1923; *L'Amico Fritz* with Tito Schipa, Giuseppe De Luca, and Raina Sabanieeva in 1924; *Samson et Dalila* with Louise Homer and Marcel Journet in 1925; *Turandot* with Anne Roselle, Armand Tokatyan, and Ezio Pinza in 1927 (when *Turandot* was a novelty); *Fedora* with Maria Jeritza, Edward Johnson, and Giuseppe Danise. As early as 1935, Merola dared a complete *Ring*, with Kirsten Flagstad, Lauritz Melchior, Elisabeth Rethberg, Friedrich Schorr, and Emanuel List. The next year he put on *La Juive*, with Rethberg, Giovanni Martinelli, and Pinza; 1937 brought an unforgettable *Norma* with Gina Cigna, Bruna Castagna, Martinelli, and Pinza. Performances such as these are not easily forgotten. "It's got to be perfect," Merola would say. "Nothing else will do." And "perfect" was what he gave San Francisco, year in and year out, rarely falling below the mark of excellence which he set for himself and his company. Because the high tide of San Francisco's fortune came simultaneously with some of the Metropolitan's darker moments, the American opera world came to look more and more toward San Francisco for excitement. The public was rarely disappointed.

When Merola died, there was much hand-wringing on both coasts. Managers and singers and stage directors alike feared that nobody could succeed the "old man." Now everyone knows what Kurt Herbert Adler, the present general manager, can do.

Adler, a thoroughly modern man, has kept the San Francisco company a step ahead of other American civic operas in productions of new operas and offbeat repertory. The company presented its first world première in 1961 with Norman Dello Joio's *Blood Moon,* given under the Ford Foundation Program for American opera; but earlier it had presented Carl Orff's *Die Kluge* and *Carmina Burana* (1958); the American première of Richard Strauss' *Die Frau ohne Schatten* (1959); as well as the American stage premiére of Luigi Cherubini's *Medea* (1959) and the American premières of *Les Dialogues des Carmélites* (1957), Benjamin Britten's *A Midsummer Night's Dream* (1961), and Sir William Walton's *Troilus and Cressida* (1955). These are but a handful of the scores of novelties which the San Francisco company has offered, but they serve to demonstrate the liveliness and imagination exercised in the planning of repertory there.

San Francisco has always led other companies in the engagement of new singers, because it was Merola's fixed policy to trace the best, freshest voices. Adler has not lagged in this, either. San Francisco bagged the American operatic debuts of one major performer after another: Inge Borkh, Rosanna Carteri, Boris Christoff, Anselmo Colzani, Mario Del Monaco, Mattiwilda Dobbs, Geraint Evans, Sena Jurinac, Sandor Konya, Birgit Nilsson, Leontyne Price, Leonie Rysanek, Elisabeth Schwarzkopf, Graziella Sciutti, Giulietta Simionato, Rita Streich, Giuseppe Taddei, Renata Tebaldi, Gabriella Tucci, Cesare Valletti, Giuseppe Zampieri—all these in the postwar era, to say nothing of Merola's great discoveries of the twenties and thirties.

Like Bing at the Metropolitan, Adler in San Francisco is bolstered by his strong Board of Directors and his tireless Opera Guild. Full-page stories in *The New York Times,* headlined "CHINCHILLA AND DIAMONDS AT SAN FRANCISCO OPENING" are no accident. Hard work on the part of dozens of volunteers has put San Francisco on top as a newsmaker. There never was a group of fans more energetic than those of the San Francisco company. Imagine, for example, that you are abroad, marveling at the wonders of the European summer fes-

tivals. A west coast woman in a cotton traveling dress begins
to talk to you; and soon you are convinced that nothing on the
Continent can compete artistically with what San Francisco
will be doing next fall.

It is California's good fortune that the San Francisco Opera
is run on the highest professional level. Adler is himself as
much a businessman as an artist. The most minute flaw in a
production does not escape him; yet he responds immediately
to those transcendent musical moments which raise the craft of
opera to the level of art. In his office, Adler might be the working president of a big industrial combine. In July and August,
when many of the European opera houses stand silent and
empty, the San Francisco offices are a hive of secretaries, technical directors, conductors and assistant conductors, rehearsal
pianists, scenic designers, and coordinators. Outside the opera
house itself, the San Francisco season is prepared in a dozen or
so warehouses, scenic studios, costume workshops, and rehearsal
halls spread around the city. Adler's company functions with
machinelike precision and efficiency. A letter addressed to the
San Francisco Opera is answered by return mail. (Letters addressed to the Paris Opéra are likely never to be answered at
all.) Because everything runs smoothly, San Francisco's singers
never complain about going there. Their contract negotiations
are always handled tactfully; the terms of the contracts themselves have always been generous to a fault. San Francisco has
always had an admirable rapport with the artists it engages;
and this happy state of affairs is reflected in the high level of
performances which unfold, year after year, on the War Me-
morial Opera House stage.

Each year the San Francisco company grows in importance.
Its regular schedule would do honor to any company of its size
in the world; some of Europe's venerable companies do not do
nearly as well. Its annual tour brings opera to all of California.
San Francisco's program of student performances, like that of
the Met in New York, is shaping tomorrow's audiences to guarantee the company's future. Adding a spring season to its
regular fall program, San Francisco expanded in yet another
direction, providing jobs for young professional singers and

broadening its already wide repertory still further. This spring season was one of the beneficiaries of Ford Foundation grants, made in the fourth year of the company's operation (1964). Judging from its past record, one cannot help feeling that San Francisco must inevitably use this money wisely, far more wisely than another civic organization which put on just one more production of *La Traviata* with the first Ford money it received. In spite of all this expansion, Adler's chief preoccupation is additional growth; he declares that his first problem is the shortness of the San Francisco season. "It is relatively short, from mid-September to mid-November. We must depend on the subscription system for the bulk of our ticket sales; and because of that system, we are forced to offer a large number of operas in a short period. We must eventually be able to lengthen the season, so that we can schedule repeats as interest grows." Like some European theaters, San Francisco uses the city symphony as its orchestra and is thus limited in the length of the season it can give. The most obvious solution is to have an orchestra which serves the opera alone; but such an orchestra would be one of the biggest factors in the budget and cannot be managed now. Adler is confident, however, that the problem can be worked out eventually.

The only important woman now functioning as a general manager of a big professional company is Carol Fox of Chicago; but her being there is no novelty, for there is a tradition of strong women in Chicago music circles: Mary Garden was the manager of the old Chicago Opera, and the contemporary journalist Claudia Cassidy is among the most acute and feared of all critics.

Fox is a determined and chauvinistic former student of music, born in Chicago and educated there. Distressed by the lack of an important opera company in her native city, she founded the Lyric Opera of Chicago in 1954, thus launching the most sensational American operatic enterprise of this century. More daring than most men in the management field, Fox refused to believe that it was impossible to resurrect opera in Chicago. She was known as a woman "more terrible than an army with banners," for Fox was accustomed to success, not defeat. Her colleagues in the initial Chicago venture were Lawrence Kelly and Nicola Rescigno, the former a real estate agent, the latter a conductor from an old theatrical family. The first performance was a *Don Giovanni* with Nicola Rossi-Lemeni, Eleanor Steber, Bidu Sayao, John Brownlee, Leopold Simoneau, and Irene Jordan, but this was a mere curtain raiser for the second work: the *Norma* which served for the American debut of the then-legendary Maria Callas. Only Fox would have been driven to present Callas in three works, not merely one: *Lucia* and *Traviata* followed, and in successive seasons, *Trovatore* and *Puritani* and *Butterfly*. Like Merola of San Francisco, Fox wanted voices; Simionato, Tito Gobbi, Giuseppe Di Stefano, Carteri, Tebaldi, Ebe Stignani, Jussi Bjoerling, Del Monaco, Robert Weede, Anita Cerquetti, Nilsson, Herva Nelli, Gian Giacomo Guelfi, Giancinto Prandelli. "Big-time, big-voice casting in the true tradition of the city's golden grand-opera years."

In 1958, Fox was decorated by the Italian government; in that same year the Chicago Lyric Opera was given an absolutely unprecedented gift, a subsidy of sixteen thousand dollars from Italy, offered in gratitude for what Carol Fox has done for Italian singers and the cause of opera. It was a moment of complete triumph for a woman who had often been warned that she could not possibly succeed in Chicago.

Equally progressive and successful is the Miami Opera, officially the Opera Guild of Greater Miami, which is the perfect model for the traditional American civic company, run by a man who understands both the glamor of professional opera and the educational value of workshops.

The Miami Opera was founded in 1941 by Dr. Arturo Di Filippi, for twenty-five years its president and guiding genius. Di Filippi, one of the most resourceful men in the opera business, is of German-Italian origin, a man who emigrated to the United States in 1913 and worked in a laundry and in woolen mills while he educated himself in night school. His graduate work was completed (including the doctorate taken in 1946, when he was already chief of the Miami operation) at Kansas Wesleyan, Highland Park College in Des Moines, and Juilliard. "Dr. D." sang professionally in both Europe and America before a long illness forced him to give up a stage career. From the theater, he turned to the University of Miami, where he began to teach. Thus he uniquely combines the various elements of European professional craftsmanship, American business method, and academic outlook.

Miami's first program was *Pagliacci* (with Dr. Di Filippi as Canio) in 1941. That production cost $1,200. Today the Miami company spends well over $100,000 per opera. The first year found the Guild struggling to meet its budget with only twenty underwriters. Now it is supported by nearly five thousand Miamians who are wildly loyal to the city's noblest artistic enterprise. Contributions from individuals are augmented by financial aid supplied by the cities of Miami Beach and Miami, from the Dade County government, and from the local Board of Education.

Although these subsidies are owed to Di Filippi's tenacity, the fact is that his greatest gift is not for fund-raising but for shaping public taste. Thousands upon thousands of Miamians feel a direct concern for the Miami Opera simply because Di Filippi has conducted a sustained twenty-five-year campaign to draw them into the world of opera. The Opera Guild has forged its own audience and educated it.

The Miami company organizes twenty annual teas and coffees, which are occasions for lectures on opera. A group called the Young Patronesses stimulates interest among young people in their teens and twenties. Another committee educates children for opera. An Opera Ball provides Miami with the highest point of its social season. After each première there is a Midnight Star Supper at a luxury hotel, where Miami citizens may meet the singers and conductor of the current production. Late each spring a full performance is given in Miami with the understudy singers performing the leading roles, the proceeds to go to Miami charities and churches. One large party each year at the Fontainebleau Hotel raises $3,500 or more, which the Miami Opera Guild donates to the University of Miami for a musical scholarship. Under Ford Foundation grants, the company has been given an award which makes possible an expansion of its annual schedule: three major operas are now given

each year, during January, February, and March, both in Miami
and in Miami Beach. These use top-level singers such as Joan
Sutherland, Eileen Farrell, Franco Corelli, and others of international fame. To these, the Miami organization has added its
program of "family operas," using young singers in leading
parts. In an expanding social program, games parties and chuck-
wagon dinners, sponsored by the Guild's Woman's Auxiliary,
have been held. New All-Star Luncheons attract yet another
element from Miami's citizens. All of this, added to the work
which the Miami Opera constantly carries forward among
school children of the county, keeps the word "opera" on Miami's
lips all year round. This is perhaps Miami's greatest achieve-
ment, for it is not easy to keep people interested in something
which lasts but a few brief weeks each year. It is very profitable
to compare, for example, the interest in opera in Miami with
that in Mannheim, Germany, a city of similar size, where opera
operates on a year-round basis in one of the finest theaters in
Europe, a modern building of postwar construction. Mannheim
has an operatic tradition going back through the centuries;
Miami measures opera in decades. But in matters of civic pride
about music, Miami and Mannheim are nearly a match, even
though Mannheim's repertory runs to thirty-odd operas per
year against Miami's three, and even though Miami depends
entirely on contributions while Mannheim is fully subsidized by
the state. Opera in Miami is anything but a once-a-year enterprise, although the season itself is highly concentrated into a
few weeks of performance and rehearsal. The Miami Guild is
an integral part of the city's life.

The archetype of the modern repertory company manager is
Julius Rudel of the highly successful New York City Opera
Company. Rudel is a one-man administration, familiar with the
strong and weak points of all his singers, constantly on the look-
out for new material which will show them and the company
off to best advantage. He is his own casting director, rehearsal
supervisor, budget committee, contractor, repertory planner;
and in his spare time he conducts operas for his own company
and manages to fit in guest appearances with other opera

theaters. Rudel is one of the most energetic and gifted impresario-musicians of his generation.

The company policy of the New York City Opera is presentation of rarely heard and unfamiliar works together with the staples of the repertory. It was Rudel who put the works of American composers in the forefront at City Opera, with his "Panorama of Opera, U.S.A." in 1958. With a Ford Foundation grant, Rudel presented his pioneer venture in American opera: ten works in five weeks, including the world première of Robert Kurka's *The Good Soldier Schweik*. In the second season of American opera, five works were kept from the previous year, and eight new operas were added. American composers had never had such a chance before, and critics and public were unanimous in their support of the enterprise. Rudel had also included such operas as Douglas Moore's *The Wings of the Dove* and Robert Ward's *The Crucible* (based on the Arthur Miller play) in his regular repertory season, together with the works of other contemporary composers such as Britten, Orff, Luigi Dallapiccola, Werner Egk, and Igor Stravinsky. A graduate of Greenwich House Music School and the Manhattan College of Music in New York, Rudel is dedicated to the new, the fresh, and the modern in repertory. He is always thoroughly excited about conducting any new opera—a work such as Stanley Hollingsworth's *The Mother*, for example—and even more enthusiastic when he can afford to put on a world première with his own company. These opportunities are not rare, for the company has enjoyed steady support from the Ford Foundation; but City Center still has a top ticket price of five dollars and a maximum singer's fee of $150, a small staff, and no frills. In spite of handicaps (compare Rudel's position with that of the director of the Sadler's Wells in London, which received a subsidy of £380,000 last year from the Arts Council alone), the New York City Opera has made a contribution to contemporary opera second to none in the United States.

One would think that such an enterprise would run free of criticism, but this is not the case. Both Rudel and the company are targets for attack by rival managements as well as by critics. B. H. Haggin, in the *Hudson Review* of Spring, 1965, wrote of

the world première of a "worthless new American opera" which
evokes rounds of critical salvos and a hail of new grants from
the Ford Foundation, which cause yet another work to be written. "Rudel demonstrated that he has a gift for promotional
ideas which bring in foundation money and publicity, but not
the gift of artistic taste, values and standards that is more important in the director of an opera company." It is to Rudel's
credit that most of his public and most of his colleagues would
not agree.

Rudolf Bing, like Rudel, is the completely modern general
manager. Thin, cool, tight, unsmiling, gray-flanneled, he has
made the Metropolitan his own; at the same time, he has made
opera exciting. Bing renovated the Metropolitan repertory, productions, and roster; he rejuvenated the whole art of opera to
an astonishing degree. Far more remarkable, he has worked
magic with the Metropolitan's money; Bing is never more than
1 per cent off his budget. He has extended the Metropolitan's
season from eighteen weeks to twenty-seven, without bank-
rupting the company. The average paid attendance in 1963-64
was 96.9 per cent of capacity, which means that the public likes
Bing's Met.

Before coming to New York, Rudolf Bing had worked as a
department store manager, as Carl Ebert's assistant at Darm-
stadt, Berlin, and Glyndebourne, and as the director of the
Edinburgh Festival. His choice of Verdi's *Don Carlo*, a work
rarely heard on either side of the Atlantic, for his curtain raiser
was indicative of more iconoclastic things to come. Bing, his
native Viennese softness almost completely sublimated by a
near-fanatical efficiency and sense of organization, was firm
in his determination to clean house at the Metropolitan. *Don
Carlo* pointed the way. It was a warning. No one was going to
tell Bing what to do; and indeed, few people have. Driven by
self-esteem and guided by rare intelligence and instinct for the
theater, Bing has proved himself an innovator; yet he knows
how to assess with remarkable accuracy the taste of the public
he must serve. Aided by an extremely wise board of directors
and sustained from below by assistants, many of whom would
be quite capable of running a company singlehanded, Bing is

more fortunate in his position than many of his colleagues in the managerial field.

Bing opened his regime by breaking up the old Metropolitan management structure and building anew. Various tasks were examined, divided into several individual jobs, and reassigned. Out of a kind of redistricting of people and a reassignment of work, came a new Metropolitan. Nothing is left to chance in this house. Rehearsals are scheduled, and singers are compelled to be prompt, no matter how much they resent the idea of having to "punch the time clock." The unholy hour of 11 A.M. is the starting time for most stage rehearsals. (At La Scala, rehearsals are much more likely to begin at five o'clock in the afternoon and run into the evening; and in the southern Italian opera houses, it is not unusual for rehearsals to finish after midnight if there is no scheduled performance waiting to take the stage in the evening.)

The Met is rigidly regulated, and Bing deplores the lack of organization in other companies. He cannot tolerate tardiness; his attitude toward his singers is often that of an inflexible schoolmaster toward his pupils, and Bing is not always tactful in his relations with them. Many of the artists think him cruel, sometimes needlessly so. His acerb sense of humor is too frequently directed against other managers, conductors, singers, members of his own board or staff; the result, of course, is that the opera world at large thinks of Bing as a cynical, sadistic aesthete. His efficiency is held against him, not weighed as a virtue. Yet most of his staff is ferociously loyal to him, and they claim—all proofs to the contrary—that Bing is loyal to them.

Like the old-time impresario, Bing does all his own casting. (Other managers tend to lean on "artistic directors" to solve their casting problems.) He also singlehandedly wields the weapons of authority in the house, for while "jobs" are spread widely among dozens of assistants and subassistants, the "decisions" are made by Bing alone. Only rarely does he ask anyone's advice; only rarely does he accept suggestions or criticism. In the words of Martin Mayer, writing in *The New York Times*,

Bing is "always a loner in a gregarious business . . . In America, Bing has been genuinely alone."

Alone in his triumphs. Alone in his defeats. For despite marvelous achievements in completely remaking the Metropolitan Opera within the shell of a Metropolitan Opera House which was physically inadequate to the company's needs from the night of its opening in 1883, Bing has made many errors. Probably the most serious of all is his hostility and lack of charity toward nearly all of the people whose paths cross his. One cannot help asking what might have been accomplished at the Metropolitan since 1950 if Bing had been warmer, more outgoing, more flexible, on the personal level of human, day-to-day contact in a milieu which once was marked by a mystique of blood brotherhood among opera professionals and fans. Artistically, his failures have fallen chiefly in the areas of casting and choice of directors and conductors; but these have been relatively few. Bing's enemies accuse him of playing favorites, of engaging singers—no matter what their merit—who have been recommended by two of his personal friends abroad. There may be some kernel of truth in this, but Bing seems generally to have made wise choices: singing is, after all, a matter of taste. Who is to say that his taste is less refined than that of Herbert von Karajan or Antonio Ghiringhelli or Kurt Adler? Because Bing seems to have a clear preference for "covered" or dark voices rather than bright voices, the Metropolitan productions often have a cloudy tone which one rarely hears at La Scala or even the smaller La Fenice. But these criticisms weigh little when they are scaled against Bing's achievements.

He is a *condottiere* in opera's war to survive. Coming to the art when Europe's economic resources were exhausted, he brought with him a tenaciousness and an ambition—a drive—which have never diminished. It would have been easy for Bing to follow the traditional trails, just as Wieland Wagner might have followed them at Bayreuth. But he wanted something better, something different, something to awaken the lethargic public to the entertainment potential of opera. To his credit, Bing is unpretentious, lacking in pomposity; he rarely talks about "art." Bing's theater is a banner-hung arena; life there is a battle. But life is exciting and challenging. Faded singers with exhausted voices are anathema to Bing: he is merciless to them, and it follows logically that he is receptive to fresh talent. Yet even the young singer is constantly put on his mettle by a general manager who is savagely intolerant of poor performances. Bing rarely shrugs off a sloppy job, rarely pardons. Unforgiving toward himself, he finds it hard to forgive others. At the Metropolitan, a first error is often the last; second chances are not handed out with largesse. Standards, in short, are not to be treated lightly.

For all these reasons, Bing comes close to being the perfect modern manager. His skill in organizing and manipulating a many-compartmented "department store" of opera stands him in good stead. One doubts that an eighteenth-century impresario could accomplish one-twentieth of what Bing does. Only one or two other managers in the entire world can match him in ubiquity and tirelessness. No one else is so exclusively dedicated to his job. Bing's seventy-hour week at the Metropolitan precludes any kind of social life at all. Even if he were gregarious, he would not have time to attend parties and be a social lion. His associates speculate constantly on when he sleeps. The two poles of his life are the opera house and his apartment on Central Park South, but wherever he is, the Metropolitan Opera is the focal point of his existence.

Being an impresario or general manager is a full-time job, though few of Bing's colleagues put in his long hours. Only a true maverick like Commander Gian Pietro Cappelli of Bologna, a man of almost superhuman strength, can be simultaneously the chief executive of an opera house and the president and general manager of a large publishing house. But Cappelli is backed by a smoothly run organization. Organization, of course, is the keystone of modern opera management.

Here, too, opera has kept up with the times. The IBM spirit demands an organization, not a single man. But a "staff" can rarely be compassionate with singers' problems, cannot sit down and reassure a singer, replacing the outstretched hand of the old-time impresario. For if that hand sometimes stole from the

singer (stealing in the form of kickbacks has almost disappeared
from opera), it also comforted him and allayed his fears and
distress. Today, all over the world, too many singers complain of dehumanized managements that hold power in the
big theaters. Their discontent rings in their voices when they
get onstage. Cold, somewhat disjointed performances are the
result. The difficulties of reconciling smooth, efficient management with personal, human contact have yet to be worked out.
One suspects that in the big art centers, where "management"
is something up on the tenth floor of an office building, the
problem will become even more severe; opera will become more
impersonal.

We may yet long for the return of the day when the impresario ran his business from a roll-top desk, with a sheaf of
contracts in his pocket. Yet we must face the fact that unless
there is a breakdown of urban population centers, opera will
remain centralized and big. This, at least, will not change in the
foreseeable future.

CHAPTER

IV

PATTERNS OF SUCCESS
AND FAILURE

Opera is viable. In the United States, England, and Canada it is more than holding its own. In Germany, Eastern Europe, and China it is thriving. In many of the Latin countries it is gaining ground after years of crisis. In other areas it is moving slowly toward success. The picture everywhere is rather reassuring.

In America, opera promises more than in Europe in the development of nonprofessional units and workshops. Many of the opera companies which functioned in 1946 have grown, and new companies have been added by the dozens. While it is true that some of these are church-basement groups, giving but one or two performances each year, yet they are alive and giving opera regularly. The only severe losses have been suffered by the touring companies and small professional companies which played chiefly to Italian-born audiences in cities such as Rochester, New Haven, Scranton, Wilmington, Utica, Springfield, and Worcester. These managed to survive the decade of the 1940's, but most of them have now discontinued performances altogether and in some cases been replaced by college workshops. Their loss, on a national scale, has been more than compensated for by the remarkable growth of opera on the civic professional level in cities such as San Antonio, Tulsa, Fort Worth, and Kansas City.

Opera in the United States is more diversified than opera

in any other country of the world. The divisions, generally
speaking, are these:

1) the big, civic opera companies
2) repertory companies
3) touring companies
4) university, college, and conservatory workshops
5) church and other social-unit presentations

The first, fourth, and fifth groups are flourishing. The most
prosperous, of course, are the civic companies; but educational
opera is assured a stable future, and whatever growth it wishes,
simply because of the enormous amounts of money being
poured into colleges and universities all over America.

The most important company in the United States is the
Metropolitan—the richest and healthiest company in the world,
despite the fact that it lacks the government subsidy which big
European houses enjoy. In fame, the Metropolitan is matched
only by La Scala. Covent Garden, Paris, and Vienna cannot
compete: they lack either the name or the voices or the polish
or the simple greatness which belongs to the Metropolitan and
La Scala alone. Neither of these theaters, however, has consistently been at its present high level of performance; they
have both survived many dull seasons. But of the "national"
opera houses, these two are by far the most successful. It goes
without saying that both are also "civic" companies, in the
sense that La Scala belongs to the Milanese as the Metropolitan
belongs to New Yorkers.

The Metropolitan has long enjoyed the support of loyal and
energetic people who take pride in their association with the
theater and care a great deal about its future. For sixty-five
years, the Metropolitan has been lucky in having general managers (Heinrich Conried, Gatti-Casazza, Johnson, and Bing)
and Maecenases (Otto Kahn, Mrs. August Belmont, and the
members of the board of directors and the National Council
and the Metropolitan Opera Guild) who were willing to work
and give ceaselessly to keep the Metropolitan going. No European theater is nearly so fortunate; and in the United States
itself, only San Francisco and Chicago can compare with the

Metropolitan in this regard. The present strength of the Metropolitan is the direct result of concentrated, prolonged, intelligent effort.

As a result, the Metropolitan is branching out in all directions. Besides extending the season longer than ever before in its new home in the Lincoln Center for the Performing Arts, the Metropolitan has launched the Metropolitan Opera Studio and the National Company, both successful and daring experiments as well as being the true children—not stepchildren—of the parent company.

The Metropolitan Opera Studio was founded in 1961 to present opera to schools and colleges, using young professionals in its productions. Serving a double function, it develops the audiences of tomorrow while training the singers of tomorrow. The Studio is the step between a college workshop and a professional stage, lying somewhere between the Centro di Avviamento of the Teatro La Fenice of Venice (which trains young people and puts them in its big productions) and the Cadets of La Scala, which performed whole operas and finally, in the mid-fifties, reached a level near professional perfection with young artists in all its productions. The Metropolitan Opera Studio averages about one hundred performances per year of abbreviated versions of such works as *La Cenerentola, Così fan Tutte, Don Pasquale,* and *The Barber of Seville,* all sung in English. In addition to its appearances in the New York public schools and the University Club and the Music Educators' National Conference, the Studio tours to colleges and universities all over the country. Many of its young singers graduate to the Metropolitan itself; many others go on to the big European theaters and to smaller American companies. The Studio is an expertly run small-scale operation.

Much more ambitious is the National Company of the Met, created in 1964. It, too, is for young artists, but the National Company functions on a year-round basis, giving its singers a month's paid vacation, as the European repertory houses do. After three months of rehearsal, the Company starts its annual tour, giving more than two hundred performances from coast to coast. Under the joint management of Risë Stevens and

Michael Manuel, the National Company is thoroughly professional: a true training field for singers and a substitute for the local and provincial repertory companies which are so conspicuously missing from the American operatic scene. It produces artists who can step directly from its ranks into the Metropolitan or any other major operatic organization.

The most successful opera repertory company is the New York City Opera. If there were a company like it in each of ten large American cities, few tears would be shed over the shortage of professional opera training grounds in America, and the exodus of American singers to European theaters would come to an end. It gave its first performance on February 21, 1944. That first *Tosca* launched a company which has managed to stay young, lively, and spry, first guided by Laszlo Halasz (1944-57) and recently by Julius Rudel, one of the Company's original conductors.

The initial seasons of conventional repertory soon gave way to works such as *Troilus and Cressida*, some world premières, other American premières or revivals of little-known works. But at City Center the repertory was not all: Halasz knew how to pick singers. Dorothy Kirsten, Ramon Vinay, Giuseppe Valdengo, Eugene Conley, and a dozen or more other New York City Opera veterans were quickly snatched up by the Metropolitan. New Yorkers learned that a lively evening of opera could always be had at very modest cost in the dusty, old Mosque which served the New York City Opera as home. It is safe to say that no other company has given American opera audiences so much for so little money, and in such an unpretentious theater. First under Halasz' management, later under Rudel's, the New York City Opera has consistently maintained high standards in the familiar repertory, while going ahead with a much-needed program of presenting new, American works.

It is obviously impossible to cover every one of the rapidly growing operatic ventures in America (nor is it necessary, since *Opera News'* annual survey has kept its finger on the nation's opera pulse for more than twenty years), but some of these cannot be overlooked. First among the civic companies is San

Francisco Opera; second is Chicago; but the New York City Opera ties for second place. Next come San Antonio, Miami, Fort Worth, Tulsa, Dallas, Houston, Philadelphia, Hartford, then Tulsa, Toledo, Dayton, Seattle, and Portland. A special niche is reserved for the Cincinnati Summer Opera, the second oldest company in the United States (after the Metropolitan) with nearly fifty summers of opera in its record.

Save for the New York City company, none of these is a true repertory theater. For an understanding of the repertory idea— so foreign to the United States—a study of the Santa Fe Opera is thoroughly edifying.

Its founder, John Crosby, was interested in repertory, not in imported stars as are Miami and Chicago and San Antonio (among dozens of civic companies). Crosby wished to offer other programs traditionally a part of a repertory theater's plan: educational programs for students in local schools; a training program for student singers, ballet dancers, stage directors and designers, conductors; and for the general community, musical programs other than opera—symphony, perhaps, or chamber music.

With a nine-week season of eight operas, the company performs three times a week. It has an Opera for Youth program (which most European theaters could well afford to study and emulate), drawing three thousand students from all over New Mexico—some from two hundred miles away. The Santa Fe Apprentice Artists Program has about thirty-five singers and five ballet students taking courses in music, voice production, drama, make-up, body movement, and languages. The company has sponsored chamber music and song recitals in Santa Fe and Taos, as well as a performance of Stravinsky's *Mass* in the Cathedral. With a permanent, year-round administrative staff; a full-time administrator for the Apprentice Artists Program; a full-time production manager, the Santa Fe is qualified to be ranked among the important and forward-looking repertory companies of the world.

In an *Opera News* essay on Santa Fe Opera, George Martin wrote that one can measure the success of the company by the opportunity it has offered to students, artists, composers, and the general public "to live operatically in their own century," and not just by good reviews the company has had in musical journals and national newspapers. "This is a vital contribution to opera everywhere in America." And indeed a group such as the Santa Fe Opera does prick the conscience of general managers who have scheduled *Tosca* and *Bohème* year after dreary year in the name of that sacred cow, "the box office." In a daring and adventurous stroke which attracted attention all over the world, Santa Fe scheduled Stravinsky's *Perséphone* and *Oedipus Rex* and Paul Hindemith's *Neues vom Tage, conducted by the composers themselves*—and all in one eight-week season. Santa Fe represents the best in avant-garde operatic thinking in the United States.

This brief glance at the three types of American stable professional companies should be supplemented by a look at touring companies, an institution which nearly died away in the 1950's and now seems to be recovering.

The best-known and best-loved American touring company was the San Carlo, owned and run by Fortune Gallo, an impresario scarcely less colorful than Alfredo Salmaggi. "Papa" Gallo, as the whole music business knew him, called himself "The Lucky Rooster." He came from the Italian city of Foggia and arrived in the United States with exactly twelve cents in his pocket, having gambled away his traveling money on shipboard. Working as a bill collector for the New York City gas company, Gallo came upon a stranded Italian band, which he booked into an empty Yorkville theater. His career in music commenced then. In California in 1911, he took over a stranded Italian opera company, which became the nucleus of his own creation, the San Carlo Opera.

The company toured by bus and train, muleback, wagon, and paddle-wheel steamer, with Gallo lashing his singers along, on long annual tours, fighting the battle of the budget in every city. "Gallo, we have only fifteen men in the orchestra, and for *Traviata* I need at least twenty-eight," pleaded a harassed San Carlo conductor. "That's all right," Gallo returned, "have them play twice as loud, and I'll give them a bonus."

All jokes about his tightfistedness notwithstanding, Gallo's performances were never shoddy. The singers were thoroughly rehearsed; each was adequate to his role. The orchestra played well (and let no one forget that it was often the proper size for the operas Gallo staged). The ensemble was often more spirited than were those of the big, prestige theaters. No one who heard the San Carlo ever forgot it.

During the forty-five years that Gallo ran the San Carlo, he also toured America with the Pavlova ballet, managed Eleonora Duse, owned the Manhattan Opera House and his own Gallo Theatre (now the CBS television studio on Fifty-Fourth Street and Eighth Avenue in New York), and served as general manager of the Chicago Opera. He was also a director of the Bowery and the East River Savings banks in New York, having been placed there by the president of the Bank of America. Gallo's business acumen was legendary even outside the opera business.

During one performance of the San Carlo company, Gallo saw his harpist having a cigarette outside the theater. Angrily, Gallo asked him why he wasn't in the pit. "There is no harp part in this opera," the harpist replied. "Well, come inside and I'll write one. I'm not paying anybody to walk the streets." A few minutes later, the harpist was playing.

Gallo gave Havana some of the best opera it ever heard, with Lucrezia Bori, Titta Ruffo, Schipa, Martinelli. The first year the San Carlo played in the Center Theatre at Rockefeller Center, Gallo counted fifty thousand paid admissions in eleven days. And anyone who ever tried to get in free knows how difficult it was *not* to pay there. In 1937-38 Gallo had six companies going at once: three opera and three operetta. His accomplishments have not gone unnoticed. He was decorated three times by the king of Italy, received privately by popes and presidents; *Time* published three feature stories on him. His annual jaunts of twenty-five thousand miles brought him newspaper publicity which could also be measured in miles. Because he was the owner, president, and chairman for the San Carlo, he provided editors with all the copy they could use. They loved him not only for his opera—no hokum attached, but always good, standard performances of repertory works—

but for his wit and ingenuity. Once Gallo sent his troupe from New York to Toronto via Scranton to take advantage of excursion rates offered by the railroads.

With great pride, Gallo looked back at the now famous singers whom he launched: Dorothy Kirsten, Eugene Conley, George Cehanovsky, Jean Madeira. He made careers. No one who heard Coe Glade's Carmen or Lucia Evangelista's Violetta or Selma Kaye's Leonora in *Trovatore* will forget the San Carlo.

The glory of the San Carlo was that it had a core of colorful, expert professional troupers who brought joy to audiences from Mexico to Medicine Hat, Saskatchewan; from San Francisco and Deadwood, North Dakota, to metropolitan New York. Gallo always played right. Even though he lost more than a million dollars at the time of the Crash in 1929, the San Carlo went on. Fittingly, President Eisenhower attended the company's last performance (1955), as if the country were officially saying farewell to a retiring ambassador.

Even after the demise of the San Carlo, other touring companies kept the road: the Charles Wagner company, another veteran group; and more recently the Grass Roots Opera; the NBC Opera company, known nationally through its Sunday-afternoon television productions; the After Dinner Opera, and the New England Opera company. Now even universities are touring their opera workshops. Opera on wheels may be on its way again.

At the nonprofessional level, nothing shows more astonishing growth than the workshop movement, which has grown from a nullity to a major factor in the American opera picture. Nourished by government funds made available through the GI Bill of Rights and spurred on by the talents of hundreds (if not indeed thousands) of Central European professional musicians who fled to the United States during the Nazi persecutions, the workshop had made a major and inestimable contribution to music in America. It has educated taste, built a public, shaped a corps of artists, and given an outlet to dozens of young composers whose works would never have had the chance to be heard on the stage of any big American opera company.

Given these marvels, it is not surprising to find that the

largest single category of opera-producing organization in America is the college. The *Opera News* survey of 1961-62 showed that a record total of 235 colleges (as against 6 in 1942-43) now list a workshop as part of their regular curriculum. By 1962-63, this figure had grown to 240, which shows that the workshop movement is still on the ascendant. College workshops have even started to tour: Iowa State University, the University of Arkansas, and the University of Maine, for example, are but forerunners in what may prove to be yet another new area of exploration in the American opera renaissance. But these, like other workshops, are subsidized wholly or in part by the universities of which they are a division, underwritten by taxes fed through state and federal channels. Ironically, some of the most voluble opponents of state subsidy for the arts are some of the most enthusiastic supporters of the college workshop movement.

For imaginative programing, the workshops have no rival among the professional companies. Because they are able to count on university funds, and are therefore not dependent entirely upon box office and contributions for their existence, they can put on what they like. We find the Hartt College of Music in Hartford daring forty-three performances of an absolutely unknown work such as *Johnny Appleseed* by Carmine Ravosa. While California Western University at San Diego staged *Der Freischütz,* U.C.L.A. offered something far more exotic: Giovanni Paisiello's *Barber of Seville* and the world première of Osamu Shimizu's *The Mask Maker.* And Indiana University, a pioneer among workshops, gave Moussorgsky's *The Fair at Sorochinsk,* Bernhard Heiden's *The Darkened City,* Britten's *A Midsummer Night's Dream,* and Walter Kaufmann's *The Scarlet Letter.* Indeed, for sheer volume, several of these workshops far outrun some professional companies.

Indiana University gives nearly fifty performances of ten works in its "Opera Every Saturday Night" program. The University of Illinois Opera Group, under Ludwig Zirner, begun in 1948, has performed more than forty operas, almost all rarely heard works, and has given scenes and complete acts from standard repertoire by the hundreds. Included in this quite remarkable record are three world premières and several American premières. A big professional company could not hope to achieve such triumphs of taste and choice, to say nothing of the honor of innovation. In the last eight years San Francisco State College has presented fully staged productions of *The Saint of Bleecker Street, Bluebeard's Castle, Venus and Adonis, Sir John in Love, The Duenna, The Tale of Two Cities, The Wife of Martin Guerre, Le Coq d'Or,* and *Orpheus in the Underworld.* One has to look long and hard among professional companies to find such variety.

These few statistics, snatched at random from a file which covers the last twenty years of opera production in the United States, gives only the palest idea of the strength of the workshop movement. Workshop performances are often more carefully prepared than professional performances. A college music department may spend weeks or months polishing its production, while a city opera company must be content with only a few days' preparation because singers' tight schedules and high fees usually preclude any longer time.

Conditions in America, therefore, are slightly better than those in Europe in this regard. The little company which goes from Venice to the provincial city of Conegliano to put on a single performance of *La Bohème* will leave Venice by train in the late morning, have one single rehearsal, without costumes and probably without scenery, at noon, then put on the show that evening. Even the meanest college workshop production enjoys an enormous advantage over such a casual professional enterprise.

Workshops foster a spirit of cooperation and team play which is now missing from many of the biggest professional companies, European and American alike. Only in the European provinces and in Eastern European and Oriental repertory theaters does one find the sense of companionship which lights the way for the American college workshop. All corners of opera are crowded with improbabilities, and this working together makes for a unity which brings these students' productions much closer to the *spirit* of the great nineteenth-century creations of Bayreuth and La Scala (under Wagner and Verdi

themselves) than the haphazard efforts of a company of celebrated professional singers recruited from the far reaches of
the earth for three performances of some routine opera in a
civic auditorium.

The workshop has also been fortunate in the high quality of
its mentors; and fortunate as well in not feeling the price
squeeze which in recent years has so painfully pinched the
American companies. In order to realize something—anything—
at the box office, the civic company has been forced to limit
itself to standard repertory which is sure to draw the public.
Thus the civic opera program is all too likely to run the discouraging gamut from *Carmen* to *Trovatore* and back to *Faust*.
True, the civic company is likely to engage, within its budget,
the biggest names available to sing its productions; but this
does not always offset the dullness of repertory. The picture
was becoming more discouraging annually on this level. But
now the grants of the Ford Foundation, totaling $1,727,625,
are making possible an expansion among these opera producers
which they could not afford before.

These grants, which go to San Antonio, Central City, New
Mexico, Washington (D.C.), Houston, New Orleans, Balti-
more, Cincinnati, Chautauqua, Fort Worth, Miami, Kansas
City, and San Francisco (for its spring opera season), are intended to enlarge the repertories of these companies and allow
them to lengthen their seasons and engage additional personnel
as needed. This may make possible an advance which will
match the progress made by college, university, and conservatory workshops. Opera in the United States may then surpass
the other countries of the world in the richness of its repertory
and the quality of its productions. For opera in America has
the potential of becoming a theater art second to none.

The records kept by *Opera News* for the last two and a half
decades show a phenomenal growth of interest in opera, reflected in the numbers of professional and nonprofessional companies. These, a handful twenty-five years ago, now number
nearly 750, producing 4,176 performances of 321 works. These
figures, for 1964-65, will undoubtedly increase at least slightly
during the coming seasons. In the United States, it is clear, the

problem is not one of quantity, but of quality. But even granted the many shortcomings of opera in America, one cannot help feeling a certain pride. American support of opera, at least in two or three limited social groups, has been growing steadily.

In southern Europe there has not been as much of a flowering as in the United States, though opera is on sure ground in the north. In the Latin countries, many cities which once had several opera theaters now have only one, or none at all. And while it is true that the European companies which produce opera on a grand scale (Covent Garden, Paris Opéra, Berlin Opera, Vienna State Opera, La Scala) are true temples of the art of opera, it is just as true that the small theaters are often inferior to their equivalents in the United States. While the Germans have gone ahead with imaginative and fresh approaches to staging, the Latin countries have lagged behind, clinging to the antiquated postures of the nineteenth century, using strictly representational scenery, often shaky and embarrassing, and token acting. One is all too likely to see a positively antique *messinscena:* indeed, many of the productions in Latin countries are so bad that it is hard to believe that a composer such as Rossini, Verdi, or Donizetti would not have withdrawn his work from the stage rather than have it suffer such a humdrum rendering.

As a result, a large segment of the public has become alienated from opera. Opera bores them: they say so baldly, and have been saying so since 1946. "We've seen *Trovatore* so many times, and so badly performed, that we won't go again no matter who sings," says the young wife of an Italian senator. Or, more succinctly, *"Che noia!"*—"What a bore!"

Since there is also a solid resistance to new works—except in certain cities such as Trieste, where there has always been an avant-garde public—opera has had hard going. Modern operas and offbeat pieces are not always brilliantly performed, though some individual groups (again Trieste is an example) have distinguished themselves in this field. Too often, modern operas are assigned to conductors who seem not to understand them, and the stage and pit sound slow. The public sits on its hands, staring woodenly at the stage, during the early part of the evening; and by the halfway mark the theater may be nearly empty. The problem of selling out the house for modern works looms as large in the mind of the French or Italian or Spanish general manager as it does in his American counterpart. But the Europeans are subsidized and we are not.

One entire generation in Spain, Italy, Portugal, and France grew to adulthood without having been exposed to much opera. This is the war generation; to them, opera is out of date. Other, newer forms of entertainment have captured their imagination. The name and face of Maria Callas are familiar, for she became a tabloid goddess, classed with Brigitte Bardot, Elizabeth Taylor, Ingrid Bergman, and Frank Sinatra in the card files of the public mind. But the art of opera itself is a blank to them. They have never, excepting rarely, been in an opera theater and have never sat through a whole performance, even of a televised work. Their whole experience in opera consists of transmissions on the national television network: the span of their attention is short—they simply don't care for opera—and quickly they begin to talk to the bartender about the latest international crisis or the neighborhood gossip. When excerpts from opera come on the radio, they often turn the dial to another station.

The sad truth is that with the exception of a few Italian cities, no one in southern Europe has cultivated young audiences as we have done in America. And for the first time in history, the people in Latin countries are ignorant of opera. This has been the case since World War II through the very period which has seen the great renaissance of opera in workshops in America.

One hundred, two hundred years ago, the church and the theater were twin sources of spiritual nourishment in the Latin countries. Music gave joy to both rich and poor: those who could not afford to go to the theater (and they were few because the theater was truly popular, catering to everyone, high and low) could at least get to know the music in the town band's concerts. There was almost no gap between operatic music and popular music: they were one and the same. Italy, especially, was music-mad; but opera also occupied an honorable place in the cultures of Spain, Portugal, and France. Now the secularization of Latin society has separated many people from the church, and a parallel movement in art has emptied the theaters. Entertainment is diversified. The opera theater now has rivals—radio, movies, record players, jukeboxes, television. Each of these has eaten into the opera public.

The French newspaper *Le Monde* (September 10, 1963) announced the results of its research on world-wide television viewing: each year 120,000,000 people spend a total of *300,000,000,000 hours* before their television sets. It is impossible to calculate the damage this has done to opera, especially in countries where inflation has pushed up the price of essential goods and thus cut an additional wedge out of the theater pie.

People no longer brag that they went without dinner to buy a seat in the gallery for an opera performance. It is easier to eat dinner, then go with a comfortably full stomach to the corner bar to watch television for a couple of hours. Only rarely now do Italians sing opera while they work. They are much more likely to sing a current jukebox hit, or to have— even in the fields—a transistor radio playing pop music at full volume. There has been, since World War II, an almost complete corruption of musical taste. In both northern and southern Europe many people are bitter about this, placing the blame on American soldiers for the waves of rock and roll, bebop, hillbilly, and western music which pour over Europe. Since so much of this is "grunt" music, almost unsingable, melody has also gone out of date. This trend toward pop music, of course, has also affected opera. Yesterday, Verdi. Today, Petula Clark.

Whatever the reason, opera which was once popular in the true sense of belonging *to* the people and being *of* the people, became during the first half of this century the province of aristocrats and middle-aged bourgeoisie. Gone were the days when it was the true voice of the Italian people. A gala première, at La Scala or La Fenice or Spoleto or the Aix Festival, brings out the jet set in jewels and couturier gowns. On those evenings, the opera house is a lively place. The butterflies flutter before the television cameras, while the people watch from the sidelines, *outside* of the theater, not in it. But compare this with the third or fourth performance of some repertory opera in the same theater. Where has the glamor gone? There are rows of empty seats in the orchestra. And can all those boxes really be empty? You check again at the end of the first act. Yes, it is true. The house is only half-full. And how many people are there on free passes? The faces are bored, and the applause polite at best. Only rarely is the cast treated to a really wild demonstration, either pro or con. Where are the people who used to weep for Schipa or Gigli? The Latin public, once so warm, has become resistant and insensitive. Only La Scala and La Fenice, consciously courting the factory worker and the student, have saved themselves from the general debacle.

Most frightening of all the symptoms of operatic sickness in southern Europe is the absence of young people in the audience. One Italian music critic recently complained that there is "no one under forty" in the theater. Again, Parma, La Fenice, and La Scala are the exceptions, for these theaters cultivate students. But at most performances, as a general rule, the youngest *aficionados* are those who were in their teens during World War II. Even those who ought to be closest to opera are often far away. The teen-age great-great-grandson of Verdi sits at Verdi's own dining table, fingering Verdi's napkin ring and drinking from Verdi's crystal wine glasses, listening to pop on a transistor radio which is plugged into his ear. It is likely that this heir of one of the world's most celebrated composers does not know one Verdi score from memory, nor is he interested in learning one. He never goes to the opera: opera is for the birds. Unfortunately, he is the voice of his entire generation.

The fault in the Latin countries lies partly with the system of state education, which includes little or no music in the public-school curriculum. When the schools were run by the church, music was a regular handmaid of education because attendance at church functions was part of every school week, and music was part of church functions. Even when neither organ nor piano was available, students sang an unaccompanied anthem or psalm during the service. And on holidays they were exposed to all the great religious music, from plainsong to the masses of nineteenth-century composers. Now, school students hear much less good music than their counterparts of fifty and one hundred years ago. They are less likely than ever before to go to church, and far more likely to tune in to the Beatles or Domenico Modugno on the car radio as they accompany their parents on the Sunday jaunt to the country.

These students are musically starved. Yet they represent the greatest hope for the survival of the theater. They are the public of tomorrow; just as yesterday's students ought to be (and are not) the public of today. The lessons which the Metropolitan Opera Guild Student Program has taught in the United States during the last twenty years have yet to be learned in the Latin countries of Europe. The careful teaching of music has never been considered necessary in the public schools. It was the province of conservatories, which were attended by anyone who wanted to become a musician. Other students were assumed to have (and need) no contact with the art.

Only under the Moro government in Italy were the initial steps taken to fill the gap. A regular music program was formulated to enrich the curriculum of state-operated schools. The newspapers conducted their own campaign: "ITALY IS MUSICALLY WORSE OFF THAN CAMBODIA" read one headline, while others heaped scorn upon "A NATION OF MUSICAL ILLITERATES." These alarms, added to the uproar over the general crisis which threatens to close nearly every prose theater in Italy, appear to have awakened the public and the governing bodies to an awareness of what must be done. But there are mountains yet to be scaled. Can the government afford to teach music when so few students can remain in school past the sixth or seventh grade? Can it afford to teach music when illiteracy is still a problem? Can it afford to worry about music when poverty and economic problems and agricultural crises figure so largely on the national scene? The new national music program has been attacked from all sides; yet its supporters are determined to restore music to its rightful place in Italian life. Students must be educated so that they can assume some responsibility for art in the community of tomorrow. The whole problem is still being hotly debated in municipal conferences, Rotary Club luncheons, and newspaper columns. Latin Europe has not yet fully awakened to the potential power of the young-audience movement, but at least the beginnings of an awakening are pushing back the shadow of ignorance.

The effects of this ignorance can be calculated by the empty seats, the indifference or scorn of the public. The famous case of the Opéra-Comique of Paris (with a shocking box-office record for 1962 of only 39 per cent of capacity) is by no means unique. La Scala, like the Metropolitan, almost always sells out. But other theaters may be embarrassingly empty. The same is true of many summer festival performances.

Part of the blame for empty seats lies with the high ticket prices, which in some theaters are almost on a level with prices in the United States. At a time when many laborers are being paid very little and are spending a staggering 44 per cent of their income for food, opera becomes a luxury. The Frenchman who spends 38 per cent of his income for food is not likely to take his wife and children to the opera at prices which range around twelve to fifteen new francs per ticket. Incomes in the Latin countries range from around one-fifth to one-third or one-half of American incomes; but the American is spending no more than 21 per cent of his available money for food, and thus has something left for other things. The middle-class American is in the comfortable position of being able to go to the theater, if he wishes, while the southern European may not be able to go, even if he wants to and has gone in the past. The opera house is left to the rich, who can pay and go as they like. The middle-income groups are now kept away by inflation. Some theaters have found a system which enables the middle-income man to buy tickets: they sell subscriptions for the entire season in installments, just as if the subscriber were buying a record player or a refrigerator. Europeans, who have been addicted to installment buying, have just begun to take the bait. Subscription lists are growing longer for the first time since World War II. Strangely, the poor in Europe have always managed to go, and they go still, reaping the harvest of low ticket prices which

still prevail in the upper galleries. It is the bourgeoisie, too proud
to be seen upstairs, who must suffer and stay away.

Opera in many cities is having a hard time keeping afloat.
Reinforced by government subsidies, which defer part of the
expenses of the largest theaters, theaters try to stay open even
in the face of public indifference. But it is a long, tough fight.
The shocking Paris Comique figures have already been cited.
In Madrid, opera is virtually dead. In Barcelona, it is fighting to
survive. In cities such as Monte Carlo and Nice, it is slightly
better off, sustained in part by the tourist trade.

Recently the city governments in various countries have
begun to assume part of the responsibility for opera. Through
their budgets for tourism and promotion, they now contribute
to the support of their theaters. Businessmen and chambers of
commerce have been encouraged to join the battle to save the
theater. But it is an uphill struggle. In a city like San Francisco
or San Antonio or Miami, the director of an opera company
may be able to count on several citizens who are willing to give
five hundred or a thousand dollars, or even more, to support the
local opera season. But in Barcelona or Bari, one can expect
little or nothing. Some of the most distinguished families give,
under pressure, as little as fifty or a hundred dollars. Most give
nothing. They expect opera to sustain itself and ask no help
from them. The habit of charity toward the arts is not in-
grained in them because they have not been asked to give
before; and they resist the idea that they should give.

Desperate impresarios have cast about for solutions to the
problem; and among others, they have fixed on the university
student as the possible savior for opera. Following the example
of La Scala, which initiated its student program nearly ten
years ago, the Rome Opera is wooing the student body of
the city. Reduced prices were widely advertised for students
during the Carnival-Lent season of 1963-64. It was a campaign
aimed at teen-agers and matriculated university students who
have recently been dedicated almost exclusively to bop, blues,
jazz, cool—anything but serious music. Subscriptions to an
entire series of performances were offered by the Rome Opera,
which chose for this experiment the "seconds"—the second

performance of each opera on the program, traditionally the poor stepchild of the fashionable first nights which call out the top cream of Italian celebrities. The seconds were going begging: nearly six hundred seats might remain unsold for every performance. The offer of subscriptions at reduced rates brought out five hundred Roman students, to the astonishment and delight of the management. It now appears that other theaters, impressed by the Rome statistics, will take up the same plan. Anything, they say, rather than face the shame of having opera die out in Italy, the country where it was born.

Can it be possible that Italy, which gave birth to the greatest opera composers, which through its teachers and singers spread the art of opera throughout all the civilized world, now finds itself lagging far behind nearly every other country in matters relating to opera production? Isn't Italy the land of beautiful voices and innate musical genius? Certainly it is. But for centuries its genius has been taken for granted by the Italians themselves. It is a commonplace of the music business that Italian singers, as a rule, are the worst prepared in the world. Virtuosity has given way to sloppiness. Italy was content for twenty years with mediocre scenery, costumes, acting, and direction, when countries north of the Alps were experimenting with new shapes and colors, new lighting, new stage techniques, and new direction. Burdened with a slowly developing industrial economy and torn by the strife of war, Italy let its opera slip behind the rest of the world. After World War II, prosperity came slowly to Italy. Germany was already fairly well recovered by 1956; but the Italian *miracolo economico* only began to roll after that. It was succeeded by the inflation and crises of 1963 and following years. Opera was forgotten in the general scramble for refrigerators, motor scooters, Fiat 600's, television sets, and Brianza bedroom suites. Once acquired, these had to be paid for. Italy coasted along on the laurels of its illustrious musical past. Then it suddenly awakened to find that Wieland Wagner had given opera a whole new lease on life by bringing into play his revolutionary concepts of staging, acting, lighting, and design. At this point, Italy's directors leaped into the breach: Luchino Visconti and

Franco Zeffirelli shook the Italian opera theater and shook it hard. The influence of Callas, too, must be counted in this renaissance. Once again blood began to circulate.

Opera in the Latin countries of Europe is still closely tied to traditional forms and expressions. The differences in quality and repertory between a provincial house and a large, famous theater are not nearly so great as one might expect—not nearly so great, for example, as the gap that separates a performance at the Metropolitan from a local civic enterprise in Hackensack. In the United States, opera is given on every level of competence, from bumbling amateur to polished professional. In Italy, the level is far more consistently professional, as it is in France and Spain and Portugal. But within that professional frame lay a picture heavy with the dust of centuries. Now, most of that dust has been shaken off.

In the northern countries of Europe, and in Russia and the Eastern European countries, opera is on much firmer ground, partly because of the heavy government subsidy which it enjoys, partly because it is founded on the repertory system of production, which seems to lend stability to any opera theater.

It seems that wherever the repertory system flourishes, which is to say in the north, opera is safe. The tourist in Cologne or Mannheim will very likely find the theater sold out; while the visiting journalist will be given the conductor's wife's seat, for nothing else is available. Berlin, Hamburg, and Munich can boast opera-producing organizations which are second to none. Bayreuth has set its mark on every opera company in the world; and Wieland Wagner has probably done more than any other single figure to rehabilitate opera in the decades since World War II.

One learns with astonishment that tiny Czechoslovakia has twelve repertory opera companies which play ten to twelve months a year. The oldest of these is the Prague National Theater, which employs two full orchestras and two full choruses, a large ballet company, sixty-five soloists, eight conductors, and four producers. This company gives fifteen performances a week in two theaters. The Bratislava Company gives five or six performances a week and employs forty-five soloists and five conductors full time. In Brno, thirty-five soloists and five conductors put on six performances a week. Almost all of these Czech companies perform in theaters which have been recently renovated and provided with modern stage equipment. Three of the twelve companies will soon move to new theaters which are now under construction. All of these opera companies receive a subvention from public funds which amounts to 65 per cent of all their operating expenses. (The Teatro Regio in Parma, one of Italy's most distinguished theaters, receives no more than 15 per cent of its operating expenses from the Italian government. Most American companies receive nothing.) The opera-going public in Czechoslovakia, as in all the countries of northern and Eastern Europe, has increased enormously since the war. Because the price of tickets remains low—at least some of the seats in every theater are priced within the reach of the poorest student or laborer— the theater is guaranteed an entire year of full houses. Because many of the theater's seats are bought under subscription plans, the management can stage any opera it wishes without having to worry about possible losses at the box office. Thus we find that the Prague National Theater can stage fifty-one different operas in a year, rotating them on a repertory system without a thought for the sore throats of a visiting star or the plane delayed in a snowstorm in London. Stuttgart stages sixty-five works a year; Mannheim stages over forty works.

The stability of the repertory system more than compensates for the lack of glamor lent by the names of visiting stars. The audience rarely hears a bad performance, and is very likely to hear a good one. The singers sing as an ensemble, which is what most composers of works performed in the current repertory intended. The level of production is usually high, often cut through with exciting shafts of imagination and genius. Moreover, under the repertory system, opera is not a sometime thing, but a regular, normal, year-in-year-out part of everyday life. As such, it cannot slip out of the mansions of art, as it has in Italy and Spain in the last twenty years. On the whole, the opera picture in Germany and Eastern Europe is more reassuring than in any other part of the world.

At least one company in this area, though, is passing through a period of crisis. The Vienna State Opera, one of the most respected and venerable organizations in the world, has been wracked for years by management pains, strikes, a lack of co-ordination and understanding between artists and management, between management and public, between artists and musicians, between management and stage crew. The critic Joseph Wechsberg laments the "badly shaken artistic morale" of this great house and the "failing sense of responsibility" which is slowly eroding Vienna's position in the world of opera today.

In Austria, where opera is the bread and butter of the people, it is difficult to hide the cracks in the vessel. Every disorder at the Vienna Opera becomes a national scandal. Unfortunately, Austrian operagoers have had ample reason for complaint. Walter Ducloux calls Vienna "the most sobering example of big-time subsidy gone haywire. As if symbolizing the extent to which routine has overtaken this once glorious temple of art, the members of the orchestra no longer wear bow ties, even for performances at advanced prices."

Ducloux goes on to make some observations about the erosion of the ensemble system which are perfectly relevant here:

"The disintegration of ensemble has made its mark on the quality of leadership found in the European provinces. The wizened, elderly *Generalmusikdirektor,* perhaps a mediocre conductor but a circumspect advisor and guide to the younger talents entrusted to his care, is a vanishing breed, even a somewhat pathetic figure. In his stead, the bold, brash and brilliant young conductor has become a glamorous figure as well as a saleable commodity. He happily relegates the chores of coaching and counseling to others, and, having little interest in singers, accepts whatever casts are suggested. His agent will see to it that he conducts only works of sure-fire appeal. It is no longer unusual to see the musical fortunes of a European opera house entrusted to a man under thirty. Yet the very superficiality of conductorial appeal has led to such a proliferation of young maestros that the public is wary."

All this is not to say that every ensemble theater is in a state of decline. One has only to point to Hamburg, Mannheim, Cologne, to any one of a dozen other German houses, to find the ensemble at the very apex of perfection, the house functioning with unflawed efficiency. Hamburg, under its *Intendant* Rolf Liebermann (himself a composer of merit and reputation), has a season of ten and a half months, in which sixty operas and eight ballets are given a total of 340 performances. With company singers, conductors, coaches, and ballet, and with the added talents of stage directors such as Berlin's genius Walter Felsenstein and Sweden's Ingmar Bergman, Hamburg draws an 85 per cent capacity on a year-round basis. Rehearsals for some productions, such as Bergman's *Magic Flute,* consume as much as three months before the work actually goes onstage. The results justify the investment: something that has never been seen before, according to Liebermann, and not just a haphazard production thrown together in two weeks, as in some *stagione-*system theaters. In at least one case, the tenor lead in an Italian house arrived *not* for the early rehearsals, *not* for the *anteprova,* not even for the dress rehearsal, *but for the performance itself,* arriving in the theater for the first time at nine o'clock on the night of the *prima,* when the audience was already seated out front. In a repertory house, such a belated arrival is not possible. The singers live permanently in the city where they perform. Only rarely are they tempted to go to other cities or other countries for guest performances. And they are far from unhappy under the system. Several American and German singers interviewed in Germany said that they would not get on the international merry-go-round *even if they could:* and these were not old, broken-down veterans, but young, fresh voices whose whole lives were dedicated to the theater. They were on year-round salaries which permitted them to live very comfortably. They were treated with every consideration by the management. Rarely were they tired: none of the top-level battle fatigue was felt here. They had nearly two months of paid vacation. Guaranteed a pension when they retired, they were living and working under almost ideal conditions. Most remarkable of all, they were financially more secure than singers who jump from one guest engagement to another, bearing the inevitable expenses incurred: travel, hotels, correspondence, extra clothing, tips, restaurant meals, costumes, telephone bills, agents' fees, postage and publicity, and perhaps a secretary.

A comparison of the repertory with the *stagione* system convinces even the toughest skeptic that the repertory theaters consistently provide good opera, if they have an even half-adequate management. Naturally, a man of genius can work miracles under either system. But the repertory theaters, most especially of northern and Eastern Europe, have proved their worth a thousand times over. Whatever is sacrificed in glitter is more than made up in the steadily high level of both the music and the stage picture.

For this reason, it is disappointing to report that so many major theaters still cling to the *stagione* system. Barcelona, for example, builds its season entirely on borrowed stars, mostly from Italy. The same is true of the seasons in Cairo (National Opera Theater), Lisbon (Teatro Nacional de São Carlos), Buenos Aires (Teatro Colón), Mexico City (Palacio de Bellas Artes) and a dozen more theaters in southern Europe, the Near East, and Central and South America. The *stagione* method even extends around to Hawaii and to Tokyo, where a company of Italian stars goes annually. However, Japan has opera performances by Japanese companies as well, and there seems to be a growing public not only for Italian operas but also for unfamiliar works. The Fujiwara Opera Company, now more than thirty years old, still flourishes. It is on a repertory basis, as are the many Chinese opera theaters, which are among the most popular and successful in the world, serving every level of Chinese society on a year-round, all-day, continuous performance basis.

In New Zealand the center of operatic activity is Wellington, which—like Australia—was formerly visited by Italian touring companies. Now the active New Zealand Opera Company, which gives standard works like *La Bohème* and *The Magic Flute*, has been supplemented by the New Zealand Chamber Opera Group, willing to experiment with *Doctor Miracle*, Stravinsky's *The Tale of a Soldier*, and other novelties. Spurred by the thirst for unfamiliar operas, the older New Zealand

Opera Company now turns to Gian-Carlo Menotti's *The Medium* and *The Consul*, and David Farquhar's *A Unicorn for Christmas*. Although none of the New Zealand enterprises is on a repertory or year-round basis, they are all illuminated by much imagination; and they have the virtue of leaning on local singers, rather than drawing high-priced international stars from New York or Milan or London, stars who may or may not fill a hall. With a growing public and a common-sense administration of the two active companies, opera in New Zealand is promised a rich future.

Returning across the Pacific to Honolulu, on the final lap of a brief, operatic world tour, one becomes aware that here, too, opera is on the rise. In its third year in 1963, the spring season in Hawaii played *Così fan tutte* to five thousand people in three nights. *La Bohème* did nearly as well. This island company draws heavily on New York singers, simply because there are not enough local artists available to carry an entire performance. But some of the major roles and the stage design and direction are entrusted to Hawaiians. The artistic director of the company is Guido Salmaggi, son of Alfredo Salmaggi, youngest of a dynasty of impresarios who have left their imprint on opera across at least half the globe.

Hawaii, which receives the weekly broadcasts of the Metropolitan from New York, has always been closely tied to the mainland operatic traditions. Thus it is not surprising to find that the inspiration and the direction come from there. For the moment, the lack of local talent is not a major problem. What is important, though, is that there is tremendous enthusiasm for the art of opera. Right now the needle points to success. Later, when the foundations have been laid, a repertory company such as that of Santa Fe will be possible. Then Hawaii will be operatically sufficient to its own needs. Until then, the islands will sustain the imported (or half-imported) enterprise and claim it as its own.

CHAPTER

V

SINGERS AND THEIR CAREERS

No singer will admit it, but the opera star, that spoiled potentate who ruled the theater for three hundred years, is an anachronism today. Composers no longer write operas for stars. Nobles and patricians no longer vie for the star's attention. The star no longer wields political power. No conductor trembles before him and capitulates to him. No crowds gather beneath the star's hotel windows, and no orchestra serenades him at night. He is no longer carried away from the theater on the shoulders of his fans, nor do the latter unhitch the horses from his carriage to pull him home in triumph. More likely he drives away in his own car, usually a station wagon, which also serves to haul his children back and forth to school. All the prerogatives and powers of the star have been usurped by other figures in the entertainment field. The pop singer has stolen his popularity, and the stage director and conductor have stolen his right to boss the stage. In the center of the opera sphere, where the star once stood, crowned with glory and jeweled commemorative wreaths, there is a void.

The singer today is in an equivocal and puzzling position. As an actor and as a part of a unified theatrical production, he is undoubtedly better prepared for the stage than his predecessors were. Yet he is neglected in the general hurly-burly of the production. When a singer throws a tantrum today, he makes news. The eruption of Antonietta Stella (against Corelli) at La Scala in the winter season of 1963-64 made headlines all over Europe. What used to be the daily bread of opera has now become the rarest kind of cake. For the star has lost his choice position. His loss of prestige has changed the whole orientation of opera.

Why has the star faded?

Who has stolen his strength and vitality?

Why has the singer slid into second place, and a very poor second indeed, in the opera hierarchy?

A Milanese music critic recently answered the first and last of these questions with one phrase: "There's nobody left who can sing." But this is oversimplification. One needs only to listen to Leontyne Price, to Joan Sutherland, to Giulietta Simionato, to Victoria de los Angeles, to Richard Tucker, to Birgit Nilsson, to any of a dozen other famous performers of this era to realize that there still remains a large host of men and women who "can sing." But they sing somewhat dispassionately as compared to their predecessors, for sentimentality is out-of-date. They sing as part of an ensemble; and in this they are a world apart from the divas of the past.

With the creation of the first operas in music history, between 1595 and 1607, the star-singer emerged full-blown. This was the *prima donna* or *primo musico* who could boast an education in music better than any available today, who could sight-read the most difficult music, who could play several instruments as well as he could sing. These early stars began to study music when they were children, usually at the age of eight or nine, perhaps much earlier, even at the age of three or four. They made their debuts early, girls at thirteen or fourteen, boys at eighteen. Once launched, the singer attached himself to a patrician household and hoped to be able to graduate to a place at a noble or royal court.

The contract between a singer and his monarch was an affair of state, and the power of the singer was proportionate to the court he served. Sovereigns often fought among themselves for a particular singer; and three times in history war was nearly declared between two states over the engagement of a

star: once, when Duke Ferdinando Carlo of Mantua threatened
the Elector of Saxony, who had stolen the soprano Margherita
Salicola from his court; again, when Cosimo II Medici of
Florence fought with Pope Urban VIII over the favors of the
castrato Loreto Vittori; last, when Christine of Sweden warred
with the Turin court over the contracts of Ciccolino and
Bianchi. The value of a singer could scarcely be overestimated.
Duke Vittorio Amadeo II of Savoy exchanged one of his favorite
singers for *two regiments* of the Elector's Bavarian guards!

Every court had its prima donna: even the pope had to
possess this human ornament to be in style. The singer, of
course, took every imaginable advantage of his position, demanding outrageous fees, favors for himself and his family,
splendid garments from the court wardrobe, lavishly furnished
quarters in the palace itself. Fees soared. An early diva, Vittoria Archilei, got ten scudi a month from the Medici, while
Loreto Vittori was paid two hundred scudi a month—more
than twenty times as much—shortly afterward. The Elector of
Bavaria paid Margherita Salicola ten thousand lire annually,
plus full favors for her mother, father, and sister. To reduce
these fees to modern terms is not always easy, but it is safe to
say that Salicola's salary would be something in the neighborhood of ten thousand dollars a year, plus all room and board
and clothing for herself *and* her family, plus whatever court
favors they could manage.*

A place at court was a lifelong job. In her old age, a prima
donna could expect a pension to assure her continued comfort
"in the style to which she is accustomed," which is usually
high style. Singers were often decorated, and a few were given
titles as a reward for their virtuosity. But in those days singing
was a most honored profession. The male star was assigned the
sacred music performed in the household chapel, and royal
figures themselves sang and composed.

During these early decades of the 1600's, opera was a royal
and very private affair. All this changed with the opening of

* The average salary for a clerk at the Vatican court during this period was
two hundred scudi per year, while a leading doctor earned eight hundred per
year. Note that Vittori was paid twelve times this amount, plus all expenses.

the first public opera house in the world, the Teatro San Cassiano in Venice. After 1637 the vogue of opera spread like fire through Europe and into Scandinavia, and then into the New World, to North and South America. The art of opera was exposed to a new audience: the people, the new bourgeois class of the Renaissance, and the masses of subsequent centuries. For the first time, the polite applause of nobility and the elegant panegyrics of court poets gave way before noisy popular demonstrations. From 1637 until the retirement of Geraldine Farrar in New York in 1922, the singer almost everywhere in the world was feted with banquets and torchlight parades. She was mobbed as Frank Sinatra, Elvis Presley and the Beatles have been in recent years. Whole cities hurried to copy the singer's tastes in clothes, food, restaurants, décor, language. Whatever a famous singer did became à la mode. This was heady wine to performers who had only recently been nothing more than highly placed court retainers. (Even the most celebrated singers of the court era, in spite of their money and power, were referred to as the "servants" of whatever noble they worked for.)

Only in France and Germany was this adulation somewhat muted. In France, for example, where the Royal Academy was founded in 1671, the singers were under the thumb of its director. Thus, in France, the ensemble system prevailed until the 1800's, and there was never the fanatical hysteria for prima donnas and stars which was found in Scandinavia, Italy, Austria, England, Spain, Portugal, and America.

The 1700's and 1800's were the years of high triumph for singers, who were absolutely supreme in their world. On the star's whim the whole music theater hung precariously. The prima donna and the primo musico had the world in their hands. The leading singer arrived in a city with as much pomp and commotion as the queen herself. The diva came in a private carriage, accompanied by her dogs, cats, birds, trunks of costumes, boxes of music, her mother, her protector, and her servants.

Note that this tradition was preserved until the Farrar epoch, when stars still traveled in their private Palace Cars, complete with Worth gowns and entourage. Even after Farrar, there were still faint traces of such glory in the air. The Honorable James Smith of Covent Garden recalls the arrival of Grace Moore for her first London appearance:

"We were all decked out for Grace's first visit to London, and I remember that a whole committee of us went to meet her. The *Golden Arrow* pulled in from Paris, and there was Grace, wrapped in chinchilla and accompanied by a whole party of secretaries, maids, accompanists, coaches and hangers-on. She leaned from the window of the train, and dozens of flashbulbs popped, and when she got out of her car, reporters flocked around her and we all presented her with bouquets of flowers. She and her party got into three long, grey Daimlers and drove away. I can't remember why I stayed behind, but I did; and as I was walking down the platform, I saw a little huddle of people getting off the back of the train. There was nobody there to meet them, and none of the reporters even gave them a second glance. When I got abreast of them, I glanced over. There was Toscanini."

This is what life was in the epoch of star pyrotechnics, exorbitant fees, and exasperating demands which reduced impresarios to tears. The famous prima donna Luisa Todi was given six hundred golden zecchini (sequins, the coin of the Republic of Venice) at Padua, plus board and room for herself and for six people in her retinue, plus a private carriage for her exclusive use, plus a private box at the theater. Her fee would be the equivalent today of $2,100 (for this single engagement), plus complete accommodation for her entourage. Add to this the augmented buying power of the day, and the total is several times what the highest paid singer of the twentieth century could hope for.

It was a maxim of the theater that the exercise of temperament was the singer's most precious prerogative. Temperament, like voice, was an asset, an intangible which catapulted artists to the heights of power and packed the theater with an avid public. The musical vehicle of temperament was the *da capo* aria of baroque opera, brilliant, florid, exciting, written to glorify the star. Little by little, the idea of ensemble faded.

The chorus in opera was reduced to a handful of singers and their music became a mere token. Opera was a chain of show-off arias sung by show-offs. Opera became a spectacle, and its singers had to overplay shamelessly to eclipse the intricate stage machinery designed by the scenic engineers and painters to fill the stage. (The musicians in the orchestra counted for nothing in this period: in *Il Teatro alla Moda,* Benedetto Marcello advises them to be good barbers, know how to trim calluses and comb wigs, and *then* to play and compose music.)

Temperament alone could not guarantee permanent fame, but it became at least a certain and sure ticket to notoriety. The royal and aristocratic audience had appreciated beauty of voice and perfection of musical execution; but the people of the public theaters wanted something more than this—something exciting and less refined: a cadenza tossed off with pagan fire; a tantrum; a fistfight onstage; a scandalous tale about the amours of the soprano. A singer, pouring out a flood of music from his throat, inevitably pleased the audience, but that pleasure was doubled if the singer had a generous share of temperament as well.

Singers, besotted with adulation, tyrannized their colleagues. The star's power grew out of the basic structure of opera itself. The whole apparatus existed solely as a showcase for stars. Even the music itself was shaped to fit the star's particular gifts, and the star twisted it out of shape to suit his whim. Once the score was ready, the singer could do with it what he liked, and the composer's only duty was to content the star. Trills and embellishments of all kinds were introduced: some were the star's invention, some were grudgingly added by the composer himself, following the star's instructions. Often the singer improvised onstage. He had complete power over the music, while the composer had none. The singer often shifted arias from one opera to another when he liked, even taking the music of one composer and inserting it in another composer's score. This musical vandalism was common practice as late as a hundred years ago. Divas such as Adelina Patti, Mme. Nellie Melba, and their contemporaries sang such anachronisms as "Home, Sweet Home" and Brahms' "Lullabye" into the Lesson

Scene of *The Barber of Seville*. At these wonders, the public marveled; but the orchestra was often left hanging in air as one of the gods of song took off on his own music, composed ad lib right on the stage while the opera was in progress.

A good example of the *bel canto* star was the Neapolitan *castrato* Caffarelli, whose arrogance and bad manners made his name anathema to his colleagues and raised him to the level of deity in the eyes of the public. *"Il divo,"* he was called, "the god." Caffarelli ruled the stage with an iron fist, which he sometimes applied directly to the heads of singers who displeased him. A favorite treat for the Neapolitan audience of the early 1700's was the sight of Caffarelli clouting a hapless colleague as punishment for a wrong note. While others in the cast were singing, Caffarelli would talk across the orchestra to friends in the *platea* or in the stage boxes. "He will joke with the men in the orchestra, hail his friends in the boxes, talk with supers in the crowd scenes, tell people that he is not in good voice, that he has a cold . . . and he will take tobacco, too," reports Benedetto Marcello about the stage deportment of *il musico*. Caffarelli even bellowed his own unfavorable opinions of the singers in the cast, until he was finally arrested in 1741 for roaring obscenities about another artist during a performance at the San Carlo in Naples. One marvels that any check was ever put on him, for the public worshiped Caffarelli. He lived like a prince, and in his arrogance was not above insulting nobility and even kings.

Another of the same stamp was Carlo Farinelli, of unsurpassed technical skill. In London, women cried out "One God, one Farinelli" when he sang. Like Caffarelli, he built a palace with the money his voice earned him, and became a collector of precious objects d'art and rare jewels. Unlike the often impoverished composers of the day, these men lived richly and died rich. So did their prima donnas. These were the famous sopranos of the era, from Vittoria Archilei, who sang in the first operas ever written; to La Todi; Maria Maddalena Musi, nicknamed La Mignatta ("the leech"); Margherita Salicola; then Faustina Bordoni and Francesca Cuzzoni, the two rivals of the 1720's, George Frederick Handel's epoch, who engaged in a hair-pulling fight onstage, in spite of the fact that the Princess of Wales was then in the theater. Ripping each other's gowns and cursing in Italian, they fought it out, triggering a general riot during which men from the audience leaped to the stage and cut the scenery to shreds. Handel warred constantly with these ladies, as he did with all overbearing singers. Once, in a fit of exasperation, he carried Cuzzoni bodily to an open window and threatened to throw her out because she refused to sing a simple song which he had composed for her and insisted on performing one of her florid *da capo* arias instead.

Singers' feuds were carried on to a higher level in interfamily rivalries. Politics even entered the stage picture; and opera fans waged pitched fights in the streets over the merits of this or that singer. Gradually in the years from 1637 to 1920, the singer came to be accepted socially (in the United States much later than anywhere else); and a famous soprano might well expect to marry into nobility and win a title and a string of *palazzi* and villas. Men of the aristocracy vied with each other to become the lovers of famous prima donnas, while these women, in turn, shamelessly played one admirer against the other to get what they wanted.

These women were so much alike in their temperament (with the notable exception of Jenny Lind) that it is hard to choose one for an example of the race: It could be Angelica Catalani, whose singing melted her listeners to tears. The gorgeous Elizabeth Billington, who Franz Joseph Haydn said had the "voice of an angel, the soul of a goddess, the smile of a seraph," and whom Sir Joshua Reynolds painted as St. Cecilia. Giulia Grisi, of the exquisite pearls and lace-draped gowns. Or Giuseppa Grassini, or Giuditta Pasta, or Henriette Sontag, or Patti, or Marietta Piccolomini. These centuries produced crops of prima donnas who could be harvested in dozens.

Or let it be Malibran, Maria Felicitas García Malibran, the prima donna par excellence, whose voice charmed the whole world; an endlessly fascinating woman, she was an artist whose genius was contested by no one, not even by her rivals. Malibran was the idol of her age, and a singer all her life, from her

debut in Florence when she was five years old to her early
death at twenty-eight. Wherever she sang, cities went mad
over her. In Venice, she ordered her own private, dove-gray
gondola (the black ones were too funereal, she said) in which
she glided through the city, nestled in furs behind the blue
curtains, her pale hand posed artfully against the vessel's
scarlet and gold velvet linings, her mind focused upon the
image she created, with her blue-trousered, scarlet-jacketed
gondoliers in their saffron-colored hats with black velvet bands.

"Thus when I go by, everyone knows it is I," wrote Malibran.
Everyone did indeed know.

Here is what the French critic Castil-Blaze wrote of her:

"Everywhere she was welcomed with ecstasy. Wreaths fell
in showers. Crowds of music-lovers took the horses from her
carriage and dragged it through the streets. Another time, she
was carried off, borne on the shoulders of her admirers. The
impresarios scrambled for her; they made her sign engagements
in advance, with enormous, incredible salaries, unheard-of up
to that time. Her journeys, her expeditions, her studies, her
work would fill two volumes of biography—and two volumes
more. She sets out for Senigallia in the heat of July, dressed as
a man, on the coachman's seat and she drives the horses, whipping them to full speed. Burnt by the Italian sun, covered with
dust, she arrives, and at once flings herself into the sea, swims
like a dolphin, and returns to her hotel to dress for the evening
after this ablution."

She was the living incarnation of the word "star" in the
opera world, the distillation of the prima donna legend, as she
stood behind the footlights, her eyes bright with tears of
emotion, while the public screamed its adoration. In all her
lustrousness and caprice, in her childishness and majesty, in her
grand gesture and her surrender to personal whim, in her little
cruelties and big generosity, in the perfect culture of her art
(for she was a composer, an instrumentalist, a painter, and
mistress of needlework as well as singer), and in her perfect
command of the stage, Malibran was a virtuosa without peer.

Since Caruso's death and the retirement of Mary Garden and
Geraldine Farrar, there have been only a handful of singers

who could ever hope to reach the pinnacles held by the stars of the past three hundred years. The public is star-starved. The *Enciclopedia dello Spettacolo,* which is the definitive encyclopedia of the stage, names only one: Maria Callas.

Callas is indeed the star of our time. Observe in how many ways she fits the pattern of the old-style prima donna (including her musical virtuosity). Her appearance guarantees success for the opera house in which she performs. The French critic Olivier Merlin, in a recent article in *Le Monde,* writes with great eloquence of what Callas accomplished in Paris. The title of the piece is "The Lesson Callas Teaches."

The lesson Callas teaches, of course, is that "the whole magnificent dream of the golden age of opera comes to life" when she sings. Merlin cites specifically the month of June, 1964, at the Paris Opéra, during which fifteen performances of Italian opera (eight *Norma,* three *Don Carlo,* two *Tosca,* and two *Don Giovanni*) were given in the old style, the grand style, with whole corps of stars to fill the roles. The singers were Callas herself, and the artists Régine Crespin, Gabriel Bacquier, Rita Gorr, Franco Corelli, Nicolai Ghiaurov, and Fiorenza Cossotto. The tangible, visible results: sold-out houses and more than *one million francs* taken in at the box office.

Merlin goes on to analyze the "magic presence of Callas." Who among us, he asks, will forget that queenly druidess of the proud gestures and attitudes, this operatic actress, this living image of the Greeks of ancient tragedies, who enslaves the public—from the orchestra up to the top balcony?

The effect of Callas on the other artists is not to be discounted either. A singer of such stature demands the best of herself and of the rest of the cast as well. Thus Callas' colleagues give everything they can. Like her, they "are handsome onstage and off, and they sing beautifully and manage to look beautiful while they sing: no more pinched nostrils and grimaces and sidewise glances at the conductor." She made actors of them all, and the whole month of opera came magically to life—as music, as theater, and as art. This is the lesson Callas teaches.

This, of course, is the lesson any star teaches. When Ferruccio Tagliavini was matched with little-known singers in American cities such as Rochester and Hartford, the entire casts were transformed as if by magic simply by having to rise to the level of his art. This is a familiar phenomenon of European provincial performances where one star and three or four lesser lights fill the cast. Star equals exaltation equals excitement equals money in the till.

But there are too few stars today, and too few of these magic nights, or months, as in the case of Paris. How many times in the last decade has the Metropolitan Opera public risen to its feet and *yelled* for a singer as it did on the night of Joan Sutherland's Met debut? Not often enough. Not often enough does a singer make an open declaration of star temperament such as one which Giuseppe Di Stefano recently made to the Milanese weekly *Il Tempo:*

"I do everything. I do what I please. I smoke. I get cold. I eat what I like. I go to bed when I wish. Otherwise, what am I living for? Singing has to be a *joy*. When it begins to be something to suffer over, then good-night! *Addio!*"

Di Stefano, with his villa at San Remo, his yacht moored off St. Tropez, his air-conditioned Silver Cloud Rolls-Royce, his mansion in New York, his Milan apartment, is today's version of the *divo* of a century ago.

"I am not afraid of anything," Di Stefano says. "I am lazy. I don't study. And anyway, what good does it do for a singer to study? If you have a voice, you sing; otherwise, it is better to forget it . . . Singing isn't a profession. Not a bit of it. What kind of a profession is this? Once I had a French fiancée. She asked me what I did for a living. 'I sing,' I told her. She said: 'And they pay you to sing?' She was stupefied. And I too am always astonished that they pay me for singing, that is, for doing something which I like to do. Isn't it ridiculous? It was logical that I got paid when I was teaching singing. Yes. At least that was a bore."

When he was asked about his politics, Di Stefano gave a characteristic answer: "I like the politicians who know how to speak well. Apart from that, I have no idea what they are looking for. And I don't give a damn."

"I love to be loved by people. I love everybody who loves me, and then I am marvelously well off."

About impresarios and directors: "That Ghiringhelli [general manager of La Scala] no longer amuses me . . . Neither does Karajan. I don't get angry about them: I'm too lazy to get angry. I'm through with them, though. Are they [Karajan and other conductors] orchestra conductors, those birds? Not one of them. Karajan's not bad, you understand, he's good. But set him beside Toscanini, Guarnieri, De Sabata, Serafin. Those men pulled you along with their eyes while you sang, you dragged the notes out of your throat and were like a puppet hanging from strings tied to their hands, your whole life depended on the dirty looks they gave you and the curses they hurled at you. Toscanini was an angel: he cut slices of salami for me and put them in my mouth, he stuffed me with chocolates, he loved me with the whole love of his soul. But when he was on the podium, he would throw me filthy looks, until I thought he'd burn me up with those eyes, and I would begin to sing *Un dì all'azzurro spazio,* and he would begin to hiss at me: 'Come on, give, idiot! Give, you damned fool! Sing, you miserable wretch! Spit out your voice, you son of a bitch!' And then I would spit out that music, and what a beautiful moment! Now, Karajan: Karajan is an iceberg. What is going to happen now to music and to opera? The whole quality of the operatic performance has degenerated, and everybody depends on the stage settings—the decorative part of the show—to save the theater. The god of today's opera is Luchino Visconti. The next thing we know, he'll grab the baton and jump on the podium to conduct *Aida.*

"We singers are like colors: we need a great master who knows how to use us. —But what am I saying? Singers? There aren't any more singers. Today, they are all just machines for turning out notes, and it's a pity they haven't got any voice. Listen:" [And here Di Stefano begins to sing, to coo, a song.] "*Io te vurria vasà.* Do you hear how soft that is? Now listen to this: this is the tenor of today, with his voice in his nose, shouting: *Se quel guerrieeeeeeeer io fossiiiiii.* You hear that rubbish? That's what they sound like. And do you understand what that means, that? It means that opera is finished. On every twenty million lire I earn from records, eighteen million lire come from Neapolitan songs. Opera no longer interests anyone. Can you imagine spending three hours in the theater, paying a king's ransom for a ticket, to see a bunch of people churning around on the stage, and hear a lot of racket, and not understanding a word of what's going on, just to wait for one aria—just one—and that one sung through somebody's nose?

"No, singing ought to be a joy to the singer and to the listener. Singing is a disease: singing is incurable. But I'm not like Del Monaco. If I were to have to stop singing, I would think, 'Well, I'm cured, and that's that.' But not Del Monaco. You know what he said to me? He said: 'I would kill myself if I couldn't sing.' He doesn't understand what life is all about, poor thing. Del Monaco is a real nineteenth-century tenor. I am different. Absolutely different."

The truth is that Di Stefano is *not* different. He, and a handful of others, are the true, blooded descendants of the great *divi* of the past, the gods of yesterday's stage. But they, like the prima donnas, are all too few, a handful, outnumbered a hundred to one by the respectable, correct, proper, perfectly schooled "icebergs" who "sing through their noses."

The "icebergs" are millions of light-years removed from the old gods of opera. First, they sing as part of an ensemble, not as soloists. They are good sports and team players, cool, detached from the music they sing, embarrassed by excesses of emotion, which they consider bad taste. They are almost without exception from the middle class, no matter what country they come from. They are almost all respectably married, with families. They commute from suburbs—the suburbs of Cologne, of Milan, of New York, of London. Their children go to the "right" schools: no nomad life for them, for they are protected from the hurly-burly of the theater which was the common lot of Malibran and her García sisters and brothers, of Patti, of Strepponi and scores of other great singers of past centuries.

Some singers, in their vanity (much diminished since the 1920's) still call themselves "The Artist" and refer to "The Voice" as if it were a sacred entity, but they are fooling themselves. Apart from Callas, Del Monaco, and two or three others, all singers today are pawns. Singers formerly chose their own engagements, dictated contracts, planned their itineraries, and wrote their business letters longhand. But now they are scarcely better than slaves—slaves to their managers, to their overloaded schedules, to the image their press agent creates, to their unions, to their own desire to earn top money in the many fields now open to them. The singer who once served the art of opera and the cult of self now finds that he is a part-time musician, filling out his days as a television and radio entertainer, an interviewer's victim, a film actor, a concert artist, the "property" of a recording company, a musical-comedy performer, the object of a fan club's attentions, and a large-scale philanthropist and contributor to charity benefit concerts and performances. If the singer is married and has children, his burden is heavier still.

In an era which has seen specialization invade every area of human existence, the singer is fractured into many parts. He is less a specialist than ever. The bad effects of this diffusion are felt in every corner of the opera world. The artist suffers. The public suffers. Music suffers.

From the period of the French Revolution down to our decade, the singer has gradually been democratized and cut down to the size of the norm, the man in the street or the housewife next door. Many feature articles appear in magazines, showing the internationally famous opera singer changing diapers, cooking her favorite dish in a modern kitchen, driving her station wagon to the supermarket, decorating her house. Does anyone remember a diva of the past lowering herself to these common denominators? The Farrars, the Pattis carried themselves like Consuelo Vanderbilt, like nobility, like queens. When Lina Cavalieri posed in an apron, the apron was designed by Worth, and cost more than a thousand dollars!

The decline of the singer can be traced through all of the last century, though even then the star retained the trappings of godhood. The growing strength of the impresario between 1820 and 1850 sapped the all-powerful singer's strength and turned him into a piece of merchandise. The rise of the music publisher robbed the star of his power over the composers of the day. Finally, the expansion of rail and air travel corrupted the singer completely.

It is the general opinion of all opera-company managements that no single factor contributes more to the detriment of the theater than the airplane. From Bing at the Met and Ghiringhelli at La Scala down to the management of the smallest professional company, everyone claims that "aviation is ruining opera because it is ruining voices." Artists used to go from Europe to America by boat, taking fifteen or twenty days to get there and getting plenty of rest and sea air en route. Now they go from Italy, where the temperature is ninety-six, to South America, where it is winter, in one night, changing air, climate, food, and time in just a few hours. The trip from New York to Rome is even more tiring because a whole night of sleep is lost during the trip. Singers travel more, study less, and suffer from prolonged and progressive fatigue. And all this is reflected in the brevity of many modern careers.

"We can't name names," says an official of La Scala, "but just think about the singers who were just getting started in their careers in 1946—after the war. They had all the promise in the world then, but where are they now? Ruined. But they ought to be singing still: some of them are no more than forty or forty-five. But too many engagements, too little rest, and jumps of three thousand, five thousand, or more miles between performances—this finishes them off fast."

The newspapers and theatrical trade papers are filled now with news items such as the following, from *Opera News:*

"April 4, 1964. If it hadn't been for a heavy snowstorm, nobody would ever have known that tenor Renato Cioni, with a free day between his scheduled Geneva *Bohèmes,* had flown off to London for a tryst with Maria Callas (as Tosca) at Covent Garden. On his return by plane, he was grounded in far-off Zurich by the inclement weather, and as there was no stand-by Rodolfo, the Grand Theatre officials in Geneva had to turn their disappointed public out into the falling snow, announcing the next night as a make-up performance. Cioni, however, apparently was afraid to face the music, and had fled meanwhile back to London, so this make-up *Bohème* was also tenorless. A frantic telephone call to Milan brought Doro Antonioli, who agreed to pinch hit that evening and the next . . . A later Rodolfo was Ruggiero Bondino."

—In a word: chaos.

Decades ago, centuries ago, when a singer moved from one continent to another, he planned to stay for months or even years. And if the rigor of travel (by coach, by early steamer) was more severe in some ways than travel today, at least the singer was not singing constantly and the menace of complete physical exhaustion did not hover always nearby. It was a rare singer indeed who consumed his vocal resources early and retired young. The annals of opera are rich with records of careers which lasted thirty, thirty-five, or even forty years. Should some of these veteran artists have retired before they did? Perhaps; but the public was merciless—shouts of "Come on, Joe, you'll make it!" greeted any singer who fell below par—and few singers had the courage to face whistles, boos, hoots, or yells for more than a few performances.

How many of today's singers will sing for thirty-five years? A glance at the Metropolitan roster shows only a handful of people who were singing fifteen years ago; and it is quite remarkable that the sturdiest Metropolitan veterans, the singers whose voices show best wear, are those who have stayed close to home and scorned the jet routes. The mortality rate—professionally speaking—is higher now than it has ever been in the history of opera.

It was only the invention of the telegraph that made it possible for an impresario to send a wire from Bologna to Milan ordering a singer to "Be here tomorrow ready to sing." Today it is worse. The impresario telephones to a manager or agent in another city, another country, another continent. "Send me So-and-So," he commands. The agent relays the order to the singer. Perhaps it is eleven o'clock in the morning and the singer is on his way to a recording studio on lower Broadway in New York City. He may even have sung the previous night. But by noon he is in a taxi on the way to Kennedy Airport, where his wife will meet him with a suitcase. He has a sandwich and a Coca-Cola at the airport. The plane is announced (on time, if he is lucky), and he is off. The same evening, or the next day, he is thousands of miles away, ready to sing with a company and a cast he may not even have had the chance to rehearse with.

By car, by train, by plane, he *must* go, because it is now possible to cross an ocean in a few hours, and because every imaginable pressure is put on him to do as much as he can within the short span of his career. The singer is a commodity, a thing to be traded on an international market and sent around the world like a traveling salesman.

This ignoble role—and the ruinous abuse the voice must take—would have been unthinkable even as late as forty years ago. The Edwardian era, Melba's era, was not yet dead, and the opera singer took a certain pleasure in living nobly, with levees, soirees, tea at the Plaza and chinchilla lap-rugs in long limousines. Lina Cavalieri, with her liveried footmen, her millions of dollars' worth of jewels, and her Worth gowns seems today a shadow from a long-forgotten era; but Cavalieri was actually killed in an air raid in Florence during World War II, and even then she was not very old. She lived with the symbols of elegance and *richesse*. The symbols of today's artists are a fast sports car, a station wagon (in the case of the suburban businessmen-singers), and a room full of hi-fi equipment. Where is the singer of today who can take time to live graciously? Even when today's artist goes out to luncheon at a fine restaurant such as The Colony or Quo Vadis in New York, or Savini in Milan, he goes for publicity, with his press agent and photographers at hand.

When the *stagione* system was in common use in the theater, the singer was assured a certain amount of protection for his voice. Few artists sang on a year-round basis because the extreme heat of the summer in Europe and North America sent most singers to spas or to the shore for a rest. Those who signed contracts to sing in South America were guaranteed a long sea voyage before their summer engagements began. Even in a repertory company, the singer was relatively safe, for though he sang three times a week, he always sang in the same theater, in the same city.

But now opera is a year-round proposition. The summer festivals have mushroomed to fill those months which gave the singer a brief respite from work. In the intervals between festival performances, there are recording sessions, concerts and recitals, television, interviews, luncheons and suppers given by the opera company's fund raisers and boards of directors. And then, of course, there are the "provincial" performances which are the bane of the existence of the Met and La Scala and Covent Garden and Paris managements. These engagements in medium-size cities which have no permanent company inevitably mean high fees for big names; to neophytes, they offer a break and a chance to become known.

The opera singer today is not much better off than the vaudevillian of the 1920's or the dance-band trombonist of the 1930's. He is not one bit better off than members of the meanest touring company of the past three centuries. These drudges traveled by night and day, by coach, train, bus, car, pushing on from one engagement to another. The singer today flies. But the killing effects of fatigue and sleepless nights are the same. Among the major singers of today, only Mario Del Monaco boasts of refusing to fly. The others are, almost without exception, constantly on the move. There are few who have the strength of character to insist on a month or more of rest each year, refusing for that time the contracts which hungry agents thrust under their noses.

Managers and agents are high-powered and persuasive. By tradition they have always tried to push singers beyond their endurance, in order to realize as many commissions as possible from the artist before the voice gives out. But today's agents are aided by the modern transportation system. The fragile vocal organ cannot withstand the punishment. For an opera singer is not Al Jolson or Judy Garland or Mahalia Jackson. He has stretched the natural range of his voice at the top and the bottom, and he has pushed it to make it big, so that it can be heard in huge theaters without benefit of an amplifying system. (If he is very clever he has also learned which points on all the big stages are the best "projection points." Anyone who has ever watched singers battle for position at the left-center of the Scala stage realizes how much energy goes into just this one exercise in the business of keeping alive in opera.) The operatic voice has to be coaxed, teased, trained, and enlarged so that the singer can cope with the heavy dramatic texture of today's bloated orchestras and the wild variety of styles and manner included in every singer's repertory—to say nothing of the four or five languages all singers must learn now.

But the voice will not take much abuse. The singers who survive are those who have iron nerves, iron will, iron vocal chords, and a good measure of luck. It is fortunate for the women who work in opera today that so many of them are able to marry successful businessmen and have legitimate children who can be supported and schooled in style. From this point of view, at least, today's sopranos are better off than yesterday's. Their houses in suburbia have taken the place of the old-time theatrical hotel which is now almost a memory in the opera trade.

The male singer is almost as respectable as his feminine co-player. He is very likely to be a university graduate, if not a conservatory graduate as well. He probably is the son of middle-class parents, and may have had a brief fling in business before "deciding to go into opera." (How often does this phrase recur in interviews with today's singers!) He has all the bourgeois virtues and pure middle-class taste. But he thinks of his life in the theater as a career. Opera today is a big business, and the singer is merely a cog in the wheel. He knows this deep down within himself, whether he admits it publicly or not. Almost every singer has a family life outside the theater which few performers of past centuries were able to manage. He is a churchgoer, a family man. He drives to the opera house himself and parks in a nearby garage. Gone are the days of the mink-lined cashmere overcoat; this is the gray-flannel era. Rehearsals, once tempestuous, are now reasonable and calm. Everyone is so polite. Rarely does anyone blow up. No one tears his hair, and one cannot even imagine a scene such as that which Rosa Ponselle once described—that of seeing Enrico

Caruso beating his head against a piece of scenery in rage over a musical mistake he had made. The conductor no longer breaks batons in two. One longs for the days when Grace Moore use to crack down with a high heel on her tenor's instep whenever he did something that displeased her. No. Perhaps Di Stefano is right: they are all icebergs. A day at the opera house is strongly suggestive of a day in the executive offices of General Motors or Siemens Electric. Confusion is kept to a minimum, and orderly schedules are rigidly observed by orderly employees.

The opera characters, like the singers who portray them, have also been reduced to human size. The triumph of *verismo* style over grand opera has had much to do with the democratization of the stage. The gods and goddesses and mythical figures of the 1600's were succeeded by the historical figures of the 1700's and the noblemen and ladies of the early 1800's. Then with *Aroldo* and *Luisa Miller* and *La Traviata* and others of the same stamp, a whole new world was opened to librettists and composers. It was only a step to Manon Lescaut, to Mimi, Rodolfo, and the Bohemians, to Nedda and Canio and their troupe, to the houseboat of *Il Tabarro,* and to the sordid world of *Wozzeck, Lulù,* and *Mahagonny.* Not a royal figure anywhere, but a great wealth of human passion, now sung dispassionately. Each generation gets just what it deserves. The point is very well taken here.

Another factor which helped to unseat the stars of yesterday was the phonograph; it has served music both well and badly. The positive aspects of the commercial phonograph are well known, but there is a negative side to the picture.

In a former age the star was inaccessible and remote, a goddess framed in the gold proscenium arch, high above the heads of the crowd. Her technical virtuosity and her usually outrageous behavior marked her as something special. An evening at the opera was an experience which could not be bought anywhere else. It had the quality of a sacred rite, for boxholders and for gallery monkeys as well. The theatrical ritual was performed exclusively within the theater's four walls.

But the invention of the phonograph (followed by the first

spate of installment buying, which made it possible for every family to own one of the magic boxes) brought the diva down from the stage and set her squarely in the living room. And not only there. In Italy, for example, every jukebox has its list of opera records, so that anyone who has fifty lire can call that goddess from her pedestal and command her to sing in any bar or café—for the equivalent of just eight cents. Accompanied by the swish of the dishwasher's sponge and the crack of billiard balls from the back room, she performs. It is hard to believe in the divinity of a soprano whose cadenzas are sandwiched between Pat Boone's "Speedy Gonzales" and Domenico Modugno's "*Stasera Pago Io.*" Only in Germany and the Eastern European community does a veil of reverence stand between the singer and his public; but there it is a matter of respect for hard work and solid middle-class accomplishment rather than for pyrotechnics and outrageous displays of virtuosity.

No small blow was dealt to the opera star by the motion picture industry, which took over the cult of the idol. Only one singer in thousands could, like Grace Moore or Risë Stevens, score a success in movies. (Stevens' film triumph, as singer and most especially as a mezzo-soprano, is one of the most remarkable of this century.) The opera singer alone once ruled entertainment. Now he has fierce competition.

Within the theater itself it was Wagner, with his drama, who stole many of the prerogatives of the star. Wagner wanted "interpreters," not vocalists. He spoke of the artist's mission, not of exhibitionism. Wagner's singers were forced to walk Wagner's own path, to serve him as their master. His influence as a reformer was decisive, as was Gluck's. Verdi, on the other hand, wanted singers, not "artists" and not "creators." He despised both words and the pretentious egoism of those who mouthed them. Let the singers study his music and sing it as he wrote it: that was enough. Nothing more was required, save that transcendent quality of "soul" which Verdi preached about.

Today the star's pride is injured. He knows that he is not the only person who profits from his fame. The theater profits as well, and the manager, and the fringe figures—the costumers, theatrical photographers, claquers. Every artist would like to be a second Caruso or another Callas. In fact, Callas' success has given singers new hope that the star system may not be entirely dead. A decade has now passed since Callas emerged from obscurity to become the only diva of the contemporary stage. Not for more than a generation has there been such a mistress of the grand effect. The tantrums of other sopranos were anemic indeed compared to Callas' thunder. Her behavior was to some extent contagious. Other singers began to ask themselves why they should not be entitled to the concessions and honors which Callas had reaped. In Italy, where so many of her colleagues had considered themselves lucky to be paid fifty dollars a performance during the years immediately following World War II, fees began to soar. Singers—sopranos and tenors especially, for they have always been the high-paid voices—began to demand the thousands of dollars which Callas, Tebaldi, Tagliavini, Di Stefano, and Del Monaco received. In the period 1950-59 (to fix rough dates) the American companies suffered most acutely, for European companies, wracked with postwar recovery pains, had not the funds to pay staggeringly high fees. Singers, then, knowing what European traffic would bear, agreed to sing abroad for far less than they demanded and got in the States. But now the high fees are international. The whole fee situation has taken on the quality of a nightmare.

The singer who in 1946 sang *Rigoletto* for $50 was asking $500 in 1951; and $1,500 by 1953; and $2,500 by 1956. This for a single performance. And many of the very top names have reached still further and demanded $3,500 and $4,000 per performance. In the case of one soprano who recently leaped to fame, the fee soared from $2,500 to $5,000 in less than three months. A staggering $7,000 is not now uncommon as a per performance fee for the top singers of the opera world.

Certainly the singers themselves are to blame for this egregious overpricing. Yet can they be censored for their demands when pop singers in Las Vegas get $25,000 per week to entertain in night clubs? But their demands sometimes bankrupt the companies which hire them.

They are right, of course, to want to be paid in proportion to what they are artistically. No one outside the music business has any idea of the work and expense which go into the training of an opera singer. Even before the singer is out of high school, if he has decided on a theatrical career his music lessons have already begun: piano at five dollars or more per lesson; voice at eight or ten dollars or even more, depending on the size of the city and the reputation of the teacher. A conservatory course may follow, or university plus conservatory—both at standard tuition rates. To this the singer must add acting lessons, languages (French, Italian, German, and perhaps Russian, now that operas nearly everywhere are performed in their original languages), dance, and often special coaching in solfeggio or music theory or history. Then he must have a coach who teaches him his roles, a stage director to plot his movements in special coaching lessons, an accompanist (even for the shortest audition, the accompanist is paid well). Because Hollywood has left its mark on every wing of the entertainment business, the singer must be physically suited to the roles he plays, a requirement frequently leading to gymnasium sessions, massages, and special diets under physicians' care to assure that he keep in shape without sapping his strength or impairing his voice.

When he is trained, he begins the search for a manager or agent who will launch him and handle his career. Today there are more opportunities open to young singers than ever before. Some of these are reached by following traditional paths: public or private auditions; "connections" provided by voice teachers; competitions and/or scholarship contests conducted by colleges and universities, foundations, and organizations such as Rotary and Kiwanis clubs, the Metropolitan Opera Guild, the National Council, and corresponding groups in San Francisco and Chicago and Miami. Some of these opportunities lead to further training; others lead directly to stage performances. But these are all too few.

In recent testimony before a Senate subcommittee in Washington, Risë Stevens delivered a harsh indictment of the American system of preparation for young singers:

"If a young American wants to learn the arts, he has to leave his country to do so," Miss Stevens said, pointing out that government subsidies in Europe provide the opportunities lacking here.

After the singer is launched, he continues to be coached, to study, to keep in shape. And in addition he must provide his own costumes for many performances (for engagements outside the big theaters, which prepare their own productions), hairdressing and personal care, a secretary, and a maid. Finally, the so-called professional expenses (mostly tax deductible in the United States) are added to the burden: managers' and agents' commissions; transportation (concert contracts require the singer to pay his own fares); photographs; publicity and the postage required to mail it; lunches for journalists and interviewers; Christmas gifts; and—final indignity—a claque, if the singer wishes one, or if insistent claquers compel him to hire one.

Because the Metropolitan has always maintained a fixed top fee, singers try to make up from concerts and extramural operatic performances what they cannot earn at home. The singers are expected to accept the Met's fairly conservative fees and consider that the prestige of singing in this celebrated theater will make up the rest of their compensation. In certain ways, it does. But every singer knows that prestige will not cover monthly expenses: in the words of Lina Cavalieri, who had a clear view of these matters, "Sweet words won't pay the chauffeur."

Therefore the singer who wants to sing at the Met and who is willing to accept the Met's fees must earn a substantial income on the side if he is to keep solvent. He gets on what singers call the "jet merry-go-round," and he rides and rides— until his voice is exhausted.

To realize extra money, he tends to bear down hard on the small opera company. Let us say that a company in New Haven (though there is none, the New Haven Opera being one group which has collapsed under the combined pressures of audience apathy, union regulations, and the demands of singers) wants to put on a single performance of *La Traviata*. In order to draw an audience, the management must announce at least one big-name singer; and in this case it will be the soprano who will sing Violetta. Now, whom can the company afford? The singer who gets $1,500 per night probably won't attract the public. So the management looks around for someone bigger. The soprano they choose will ask $5,000 for her night's work. She may not want to attend any rehearsals, either in New York or in New Haven, because she is tied up with performances right up to the minutes of her Connecticut engagement. So she will arrive in New Haven (tired) on the day of the performance, or perhaps the night before. She may glance around the stage to see where the props have been put, or have a brief interview with a stage director. If the company is lucky, she may have sung somewhere before with the same cast or conductor. In this case, things may go very well. If not, she may sing the part without rehearsal and with a cast and conductor whose work she does not know.

Once the soprano is signed up with a contract, the New Haven company will try to find a tenor for somewhere in the $1,000-$1,500 price range, and a baritone for $1,000 to sing Père Germont. To these leads the company must add an orchestra and conductor, chorus, scenery, costumes, a stage director, a chorus manager, stage hands, and other assorted personnel. If it engages top-price artists right down the line, the production costs (like those in Miami, Florida, discussed in Chapter III of this book) will run over $100,000. But it is possible to get by on half of that, or less.

If the weather is perfect and the soprano famous enough, the company stands a good chance to break even, or perhaps make a profit. If, through some whim, the public would rather hear Price or Sutherland or Nilsson instead of the soprano who has been engaged, the company may take a small loss. But if bad weather strikes *and* the public is indifferent, the New Haven Opera is likely to lose thousands of dollars and end up completely bankrupt.

The singer does not care. Unlike Maria Malibran, who performed benefits *at no fee* to save the director of a Venetian theater (who in gratitude renamed his theater in her honor), the modern singer has problems of her own which keep her quite apart from the managements of small companies. The famous modern artist saves her smiles for the big birds. She arrives in New Haven as scheduled. She is busy and cannot possible postpone the performance, as Europeans regularly do. Tomorrow she must be in New York, while the tenor will take off for San Antonio, together with the stage director and the conductor. Next week will find these singers even more widely dispersed, for the soprano has an engagement in Milan, while the baritone has been signed up for five *Traviatas* in Barcelona. So the company in New Haven must put on its *Traviata* tonight. If the theater is not filled, if the company sustains too many losses, it will not stay in business long. Inevitably, these small professional companies blame high-priced singers and unions for their troubles. Their European counterparts, bolstered by national or city subsidies, are in a much more comfortable position, for the small American professional company must compete not only with records, radio, movies, and television, but also with workshops which *are* subsidized by the state or federal government.

As European companies have become gradually able to pay very high fees—often higher than those paid in the United States—singers have become increasingly contemptuous of the small American company, although they are always glad to work for the high-paying outfits such as Miami, Dallas, San Antonio, or San Francisco. (The reverse is not true, however: American singers always consider themselves lucky to get an engagement from a small European opera house where, they believe, they get more and better experience.) There are scores of examples on record of leading singers—European and American alike—canceling an engagement with a small American professional company at the last minute: perhaps the day before the performance, or three or five days before. The company in Europe, where distances are small, can telephone for a replacement from a nearby city. In America it is far more difficult. If the company fills the role with an unknown singer, the public may not come to the performance. If a substitute is announced at the last minute, from the stage, the audience will feel outraged and cheated. They may not ask for their money back, but they will be wary of paying for tickets the next time the company schedules an opera. The company management is trapped, but it can do nothing to protect itself against its leading singer's defection. Imagine, then, the company's rage when it discovers that its high-priced Violetta, who cabled from Milan that she was too sick to keep her engagement in New Haven on October 28, did in fact sing in Venice on that very same night, apparently in perfect health.

This type of abuse has always been common in the music business; but when it took a week to travel to Rome, say, from Milan, singers were less likely to sign contracts unless they were fairly sure of being able to keep the engagement. Now the jet airplane makes them think that they can do almost anything (as witness Renato Cioni's signing with London and Geneva for consecutive nights—and this is but one example among thousands which could be cited) and last-minute defections based on "ill health" menace every company in the world.

Opera companies which have been thus deceived find it difficult to forgive the singer who has put them in such an embarrassing spot, especially if the soprano is a young upstart worth $500 per performance but asking $2,000 so as not to be left out of the fee race.

In the past five years fee raises have become a real threat to every opera company. Managements have taken some steps toward their own kind of union, which may protect them against the singers' abuse of power. Wishing to shield their budgets from the raids of overpriced singers, they have tried to formulate a kind of price-fixing agreement—even on an international scale. It would work like this: the management of the six or seven biggest opera companies would agree on a top fee, then hold the line against all demands above the figure. Singers, of course, cry "foul," fearing the day when their fees will be as firmly regulated and as closed to negotiation as the price printed on a box of detergent.

Outraged at the possibility that even this last weapon may be taken from them, singers have reacted, some voicing protests through their unions, others protesting in person to opera-house managements. Singers have always had a long list of grievances—some very real—against managements. One has only to linger backstage to hear them all: too many rehearsals; too many performances; too many interviews; too many costume fittings; too many prolonged sittings with the house photographer; too many social obligations forced on them by opera-company executives who love to increase their own prestige by exhibiting their singers as if they were prize horses.

The American opera companies are singled out as a source of particular offense in most of these areas; for here private fund-raising committees depend on the big-name singers to help them in their campaigns. Social events figure heavily in their plans: teas, receptions, champagne suppers, each of which must have a famous singer (at least one) as its drawing card. Thus another burden is added to the killing schedule which most modern singers have to maintain.

The human voice is the most fragile of all instruments. It cannot be replaced. Once damaged, only rarely can it be mended. Yet the singer is confronted with whole squadrons of people who demand of him more than he ought to give. He must constantly sing higher than his eighteenth-century predecessors, for our A is tuned to 440 vibrations, while the A of Mozart's time was at least a full half-tone lower at 435 vibrations. This puts unrelenting, day-to-day strain on the voice, by pitching every note sung a half-tone high.

His own heart tells him that he ought to be earning more, trying harder. Taxes are high, in Europe as in the States. Hotel rates all over the world have become exorbitant; and a singer with any kind of reputation at all *has* to go to the best hotel. Restaurant meals have leaped in price. Thus even the singer who earns $3,500 per night may find that that big sum has dwindled to virtually nothing by the time he pays all his expenses. The public imagines that every singer in opera lives in film-star splendor. Nothing could be farther from the truth. Most singers live fairly modestly. They pay dearly for their glory and find out that not much money is left over for their personal whims. More than one Metropolitan soprano has bought her mink coat at a second-hand fur shop.

Singers now feel hounded on all sides. In Caruso's era, and for at least two centuries before it, opera companies worked hard to please their stars. Even as late as the decade which preceded World War II, singers were handled with kid gloves. But now singers find management diffident and remote, overwhelmed with the details of running a huge business operation. A general manager's eye must scan the whole picture: he no longer has time to coddle stars, and may in fact be very rude to his leading singers. The singer feels hurt. He feels that an old and sacred bond has been ruptured and that the old operahouse camaraderie is dead.

Out of all this upheaval a new theater has been born. It is the theater of the ensemble, the massing of forces, the coordinated effort, the credible stage picture, the modern drama, the clockwork schedule which is mimeographed and posted all over the opera house. Very probably, the singer will never again receive the handwritten invitations to rehearsals which managers even in the 1920's wrote to their stars. The opera theater today seems to be perfectly wedded to the hurried tempo of contemporary life. It is the world of Telstar, of supersonic jets, of international exchange. We do not yet know what it will be in the long run, whether opera can ever again serve art and the star and the public. Only time will tell.

CHAPTER
VI

THE PROVINCES

The bare truth is that European provincial opera houses are still the best training ground for young singers, just as they were in Farrar's and Mary Garden's day. Careers are born in the provinces, whether in Germany, Italy, France, Yugoslavia, or even on the provincial touring circuit which takes young Americans to Australia or New Zealand with Italian touring companies.

The young singer studies in Cincinnati, let us say, then he graduates to New York, perhaps to a private teacher, perhaps to a conservatory. Eventually he will be counseled to try Europe. He finds a European teacher or coach, who in turn puts him in the hands of an impresario or agent. The next step is a provincial debut performance, that first Mimi or Edgardo in Como, Piacenza, Brescia, Bordeaux, Leeds, Bielefeld, or Coburg.

The singer arrives by train in the provincial city, his costumes in his suitcase, his score in his briefcase, and his heart in his throat. It is a tradition of opera that he goes directly to the theater. There he meets his first conductor, his first prompter. He is shown around the house. There is the stage, there are the footlights. And out there, across that "mystic gulf" where the orchestra sits, out there will be those faceless faces which are his first public. He has reason to be frightened.

The management has reserved a hotel room for him, usually in a second-class hotel, because the singer pays his own lodging. Would the singer like to go there first, unpack, and then report for rehearsal this afternoon at four? When the young singer comes back to the house for his first rehearsal, his career begins. Here begins his rapport with the composer (dead or alive), with other singers, with the orchestra, with the conductor and stagehands and scenic designer and stage director. All of these will work to make him the artist he will eventually become. It is the singer's success *within this ensemble* (and not as a hard-riding, temperamental loner) which determines his fate in the opera world of today.

In the provinces there is a sense of intimacy which is rarely achieved in the big theaters. The members of the cast become friends. There is a warm camaraderie which unifies the working cast and the staff. The singer learns for the first time what a complex business it is to get an opera onstage. He gains a respect for his colleagues.

Because provincial cities are small, there is usually one café near the theater where everyone goes for coffee, one restaurant where the cast eats together. The cast are almost all young, filled with enthusiasm and energy and evangelical fire. When they are not singing opera, they are talking about it. Rarely a word about their backgrounds, their families, their pasts. They talk only of the performances they have heard, the idols they have worshiped. They talk about the performance they are working on: this scene needs more work; that passage is difficult; here the orchestra is a little slow; there the cues can't be heard. If the conductor is an older man, he sets their minds to rest. They will all work harder at it, and it will all come out perfectly. If the conductor is young, there is less certainty about it all; but everyone pulls together to polish the production.

Rehearsals follow rehearsals. Life is all opera. Although many provincial cities are beautiful, far more beautiful than the huge, sprawling metropolitan *massifs*, the singer rarely has time for any sightseeing. His schedule is too tight to permit more than a brief stroll around town, or a little window-shop-ping. If he somehow finds time to buy a tube of toothpaste, he is lucky. At the end of the day the singers, and the conductor who will lead them through this trial by fire, have a light supper together. Then off to the hotel to bed, with one last glance at the score before turning out the light.

This is total dedication. At this lap of the race, the young singer is an unknown. He has no television engagements, no journalists following him, no press agent on the telephone— international, from New York. He is very close to what opera was three hundred years ago. First, because the provincial city is similar in size to the cities of the seventeenth and eighteenth centuries: the monster population centers of millions are modern phenomena. Secondly, because provincial people still think of opera as entertainment. Often there are no other theaters in the city (not as in New York, Paris, Milan, London, Rome, where one can choose from a list of twenty productions). The two or three movie houses in a provincial city often show second-run pictures; so the opera house is still held in high esteem. There is no competition from night clubs, dance halls, musical comedies, revues, recitals. Thirdly, because opera in the provinces is an integral part of provincial life. The theaters have a high rate of attendance: the average attendance in Italian provinces is 70 per cent, but for standard operas it runs higher. In German theaters it runs 80 per cent for standard operas, 65 per cent for novelties. Also, in the provincial city much of the public walks to the theater. Strange as it sounds, this has a profound psychological effect on the audience as well as on the performance. The opera house is something close to home, like the grocery, the newspaper vendor, the church around the corner. When it lies within an easy walk from one's house, the theater is a part of the daily life of the city. The audience is a family. When the night of the performance arrives, there is a sort of comfortable, living-room feeling which pervades the theater.

The young singer who was so frightened two weeks ago has by now gained a little confidence in himself. He has assessed his colleagues and his conductor, and knowing what to expect from them, he can relax and put himself into his part. If he makes a mistake, he knows it will not mean the end of his career, for this is not New York or Milan. There are no big-time critics out front, laying for him. He can give his best performance, precisely because he is not wracked with big-city nerves. And a long series of these best provincial performances —three or five years, say—is the most solid foundation for a long career.

For all these reasons, there is no substitute for opera in the provinces. It has not been superseded by any other form of theater. Provincial opera houses continue to be the indispensable first step for any singer who hopes to reach the top. Here, and here alone, the singer gains the confidence and experience he will need if opera is to be his career for life. Singing ten Rodolfos in the province is *not* the same as singing ten Ruizes at the Metropolitan. The young artist whose first stage experience is gained singing secondary roles in a big theater is not as soundly prepared for a long professional career as the singer whose first experience is in leading roles in the provinces. The histories of Giulietta Simionato at La Scala and James Mc-Cracken at the Metropolitan give us two excellent examples of the dead end to which secondary roles in a big theater can lead. Both Simionato and McCracken would surely have been doomed forever to singing minor parts had they not made the break and gone away to start almost over again in order to reach the top. "Once a *comprimario*, always a *comprimario*," managers say cynically. Almost to a man they refuse to give lead roles to singers who have started with second parts. "Get that *comprimario* mentality, and nothing will make you a star," they warn their young singers. The singer who begins with a lead role in even the smallest and most unimportant provincial city is leagues ahead of the singer who accepts a small part in order to get into a big theater.

Most of the routes open to the American singer who stays at home lead to small parts in big theaters because here there is no provincial opera in the real sense. The New York City Opera is a notable exception to this general rule, for it puts young people directly into leading roles with the result that many of this company's alumni then go on to leading roles at the Metropolitan. But the other American professional companies are not all so generous. They import their leading singers from New York or from Europe. Thus the young American artist finds almost all doors closed to him in his own country.

He must turn to nonoperatic singing, and lose precious months or years. A coloratura such as Laurel Hurley, for example, played in operetta until she could secure a guest appearance as Norina in the Hartt College *Don Pasquale* in Hartford. Mary Costa did television commercials. Other equally gifted singers are buried in night clubs or in Broadway musical-comedy choruses, and many will never escape.

The only rays of hope on the American opera horizon at the moment are the growth of companies such as the National Company of the Metropolitan, the spring opera of San Francisco, and the use of young people in special works—such as Miami's productions, which are called "family operas" and are intended to give beginning artists a chance. These programs are the necessary intermediate step between the conservatory or private teacher workshop and the professional big time. Underwritten as some of these are by Ford Foundation grants, they fill the great gap in the American operatic structure. If they are nourished, the United States will have a mechanical apparatus, from the first vocal lesson to the highest and most polished professional production, second to none in the world.

Because it had had good theater for three hundred years, the Teatro Regio in Parma is the provincial theater par excellence, the finest monument of a region which is commonly called "the land of opera." Here were born Toscanini and Verdi, Ildebrando Pizzetti and Ferdinando Paer, Giovanni Bottesini, Gaetano Bavagnoli, Emmanuele Muzio, Renata Tebaldi, and a whole host of less famous musicians. Parma, which lies along the Roman Via Emilia in the Po Valley, is said to be the most musical city in the world. Nearly every one of its 150,000 citizens is an expert on opera.

The operatic traditions of the city go back to the Farnese dukes (1545-1731) and cover the reigns of the enlightened Spanish Bourbons (1749-1802) and of the Archduchess Marie Louise, second wife of Napoleon I, who governed Parma with "sweetness and moderation, and beautified the city." Parma has always been the "Athens of Italy," a captivating and gracious place. But its opera-going public is (and always has been) bloodthirsty, from the panthers in the top balcony down to the mink-jacketed aristocrats in the first-tier boxes.

The Teatro Regio, built in 1829, succeeded an early and famous theater, the old Teatro Ducale, which was itself only one of the ten theaters built in Parma to satisfy the public's hunger for opera. The major artists of every epoch have polished Parma's taste. Parma brags that its orchestra members could perform as concert soloists anywhere. This anecdote about Verdi admirably illustrates the pride Parma takes in its musical traditions:

Late in Verdi's life, when he had made his peace with La Scala after a feud which lasted for decades, the composer was in Milan rehearsing for the première of one of his operas. At a certain point in the score, a double-bass player in La Scala's orchestra protested that one of Verdi's phrases was unplayable.

"Unplayable?" Verdi said. "We'll see about that. Let it go until tomorrow."

Verdi returned to his hotel and telegraphed to Eustachio Pinetti, a musician from Parma. "Come at once and bring your double-bass," Verdi wired.

The next day found Pinetti at La Scala. When the orchestra men saw the big, ruddy farmer from the provinces, they began to snicker. But soon they were applauding, for Pinetti played the "unplayable" passage perfectly.

"That's how they play in Parma!" shouted Verdi triumphantly, from the stage.

Parma hasn't changed. The public knows every operatic aria and recitative from memory, and can sing every duet, sextet, trio, or ensemble *in parts!* Laborers and factory workers get together after work to sing: from this custom, which dates back across centuries, grew the famous Parma singing clubs—each a ferocious rival of the others. Hotel porters sing in Parma. Waiters in restaurant kitchens harmonize with the cook. Housemaids sing as they beat carpets over the balcony railings. Farmers sing in their fields. As in the Appalachian Mountains of Kentucky, Virginia, and West Virginia, nearly everyone plays one or more instruments. Indeed, it was for dilettante musicians of the Philharmonic Society of Busseto (population: 2,000) near Parma that Verdi began to compose. If any city in the world deserves to be called the capital of opera, it is Parma.

The Teatro Regio itself was commissioned by the Archduchess Marie Louise. It opened on May 16, 1829 with Bellini's *Zaira,* which was composed expressly for the purpose. The Parmigiani killed the opera in one performance. It was not heard again. The Regio is an imposing classic structure which is in perfect harmony with Parma's serene beauty. The severe portico of the theater is sustained by a long row of unadorned Ionic columns, above which five large Empire windows and a semicircular skylight illuminate the interior. Two sculptured masks in half-relief bear the emblems of tragedy and comedy; they are the only frills on the façade. Inside, the elliptical auditorium, elegant in white and gold, seats fifteen hundred self-appointed critics of opera.

The Regio has lived through a long chain of golden ages: from the year of its opening until World War I, it was in every way the equal of the Regio of Turin, the Comunale of Bologna, the Carlo Felice of Genoa, the Apollo of Rome, the San Carlo of Naples. Often it surpassed La Scala, for in addition to its distinguished musical ensemble, the Regio boasted the most advanced stage machinery of the age.

Here Verdi directed his *Nabucco* and, a whole lifetime later, his *Aida.* The two productions are, by tradition, two of the artistic landmarks of Verdi's life. But Verdi was not the only composer to bring his works to Parma. Amilcare Ponchielli (a native of nearby Cremona, which also produced the Stradivari and Guarnieri) gave his *La Gioconda* and *Marion Delorme* at the Regio. Umberto Giordano put on *Andrea Chénier* here, Pietro Mascagni, *L'Amica,* and Puccini, *La Bohème.* Each of these composers wanted to be certain that his work was given the best possible performance for the world's most difficult audience.

The annals of the Regio are rich in anecdotes about the Parma public. No audience ever looked more gentle and less

dangerous. With their bright eyes and red cheeks and lisping
accent, the people of Parma are the *putti* angels in Renaissance
friezes. But each of those cherub faces masks a tiger. No theater
has ever given its artists a harder time.

Many are the singers who have been run out of the city by
the Parma audience. During the Carnival season of 1816, the
tenor Alberico Curioni was engaged for another *Zaira* (by
Vincenzo Federici, not the Bellini work of the same name).
When the audience greeted him with whistles and boos and
shouts, Curioni turned on them, cursing them for their in-
gratitude. The public roared for vengeance. To restore order,
a police inspector came out before the curtain to say that
Curioni had been arrested and that a ballet would replace the
opera, on which the curtain had been rung down. At the end of
the ballet, Curioni returned to the stage to apologize to the
public. Then and only then was the performance allowed to
resume. Two months later, during the last opera of the season,
Curioni decided to have his revenge. He walked to the footlights and began to whistle to the public—the whistle being
the lowest level of discourtesy in Italian theater, since Bronx
cheers are against the law and punishable by arrest. Again a riot
ensued which the police had to subdue. Curioni was again
arrested. He served eight days in jail, then was escorted to the
frontier of the duchy and exiled. Yet Curioni was a tenor of
considerable reputation, indeed, even of some distinction.

The following season, when the soprano Carolina Gentili was
hooted offstage, the opera in which she was singing was replaced by another work. But this, too, was whistled off; and
the manager then brought back Gentili in still a third work to
finish the season.

After the failure of opening night in 1818, the police shut
down the theater and sent the impresario to jail "for offending
public taste," as the charge against him read. He was finally
released on the condition that he improve his program. But
when he failed a second time, he lost his job.

Not even Verdi, a native son, was spared. In the 1846-47
Carnival season, the public became bored with *Ernani*, which
was given several evenings in a row, as was the custom in that

time. On the night of February 13, the public set up such a howl just before the performance that the impresario withdrew the first act of *Ernani* from the boards and substituted the prologue of Verdi's *Attila*, which had been written for La Fenice in Venice. After this, the singers performed several excerpts from the second act of *Ernani*; but the audience began to give signs of disapproval—the throat-clearing and the famous "Parma groan" which even today strike terror into singers' hearts. The baritone was then brought out alone to sing an aria from Gualtieri Sanelli's *Luisa Strozzi*, with the chorus following him as best it could. Then came the ballet, and after it came the third act of *Ernani*. It is a tradition of the Italian theater that the third act is fatal. By the third act, the evening is late, the artists tired, and the public bored. The most frequent disasters, onstage and off, fall during the third act. So it was on this February 13. As the orchestra got underway with *Ernani*, the public broke into demonic howls and whistles and shouts of *"Basta! Basta!"* The police commissioner came onstage to order silence; but he, too, was whistled off. The curtain was then rung down and the public was turned out into the streets to continue the riot there. So ended the 1846-47 season in Parma!

All of this goes to prove not only how difficult Parma was, but also how spontaneous opera once was—and how slick it has now become. Opera was once performed at about the same level as a burlesque-house Saturday matinee. The audience responded as the audience responds now at the Old Howard in Boston and other burlesque theaters around the States. But now, at the big opera houses, how different, how polite it all is!

Parma, however, has not changed very much, and that is why it is of special interest here. When an unfamiliar work is on the program, the audience is reasonable and fairly charitable. A slight slip from pitch or a loss of pace in the orchestra provokes only prolonged throat-clearing and a few resigned sighs. But when the listeners are on familiar ground, in *Carmen* or *Rigoletto* or *La Traviata*, anything can happen.

Fifty years ago the celebrated Parma tenor Italo Campanini forgot his lines during a performance at the Regio. "Hey,

Campanèn, this is how it goes," shouted someone in the top balcony. And the entire theater took up the tenor's music, singing the whole aria perfectly. This they can do (and still sometimes do) with any popular piece of operatic music.

The people of Parma know the personal history of every singer who goes there. They know where he is from, whom he has studied with, where he made his debut, where he has sung recently. They also know how much he is paid. Major artists are judged more severely than beginners, because they are more highly paid. Toward a tyro the public is likely to be charitable. But toward a famous singer they have no mercy. To be sure, they are more polite than they were a hundred years ago. Then, hardly a week passed without a riot. In 1864, the tricolor flag of the new unified Italy had to be brought out to quell a demonstration at the Regio. But decades have passed since the last time the Parma public threw chairs onstage as a sign of displeasure! Today they kill with groans, hisses, whistles, and shouts. No other theater has run down its curtain in midperformance more frequently than the Regio: on some evenings, the public has interrupted the performance six or seven times.

A recent demonstration took place there three years ago, when a hapless tenor, hooted down, was escorted to the Milan train by the police. With his topcoat thrown over his costume, he stepped from the Regio stage door to face a mob which had gathered there. As the people poured their scorn over him, a local philosopher observed that this tenor was lucky. In Verdi's day it was worse: "Then they stood out here with clubs and sickles." In 1965, a harassed American baritone left the theater after cursing the audience from the stage and throwing a candlestick toward the orchestra.

The Regio belongs almost completely to the people of Parma. After the unification, when the ducal orchestra was disbanded, it seemed that the Regio would have to close. But Parma was too proud to let its theater expire. The traditional Carnival season was kept up, excepting from 1892-94. In those years, an economy drive on so-called luxury items darkened the Regio.

But even then, modest Carnival seasons were given in smaller theaters.

Parma, however, wanted the Regio. A group of citizens wished to reopen the theater in 1894-95, but the city opposed this financial burden. The question was put to a city-wide referendum, in which the people voted overwhelmingly to keep the Regio open. From that time on, music has flourished.

Today the Regio is an object of civic pride. It is, and has been, maintained by the people of the city. Americans commonly believe that all the theaters of Europe are kept running with large government subsidies, but this is not always the case. Parma, for example, receives only about 15 per cent of its funds from the Italian government. Thirty-three per cent is given by the city of Parma from public funds. The rest is covered by box office and subscriptions.

The theater is run by a Parma businessman, not an artist. Its general manager, Dr. Gaetano Negri, is a pharmacist, the owner of a local drugstore. With a staff of only seven people, he manages to keep his budget balanced and his theater full. Negri uses a good deal of imagination in his planning of roster and repertory. "I, like a good pharmacist, try to concoct the right mixture of old and new to educate the public." Thus the Regio bills not only standard works, but offbeat operas as well. "Opera here is gaining ground every day, thank God!" says Negri. "We have full houses, and a program which is richer and more interesting every year. Once it was impossible to give anything but repertory operas. Now Parma welcomes unknown works and new composers." In Italy, where the public is notoriously resistant to unfamiliar operas, this fact itself is worthy of special attention.

The public here grows, while in other cities it has fallen away. The interest in opera is certainly owed in part to Parma's musical traditions. But how to account for an *increased* interest in opera? The management of the Regio believes that the new prosperity brought by the Italian "economic miracle" has benefited the theater. "Fifty years ago, large numbers of people here went hungry every day of their lives. There was real misery, not just in the south, as everyone believes. Even then,

people would make a real sacrifice in order to go to the theater
once in a while. The gallery seats were very cheap, of course.
Now it is easier to go to the theater than ever before, and
more pleasant, too. People have new clothes, so they can be
seen in public." (The management of the Teatro Verdi in
Trieste made the same observation, adding that the top balcony
is less and less full every year, because people are now well
enough dressed and prosperous enough to be able to afford
seats in the lower parts of the house.) "Unfortunately, some
people come only for snob reasons. But most people come because the theater is entertainment: people like to come."

This is perhaps the key to opera's success in Parma. People
like to come. They do not buy tickets because it is a civic duty,
as in some American cities. "They buy because they enjoy what
we put on."

The Regio, like all provincial theaters, seems to bring out
the best in a singer. Musicians on all levels declare that in spite
of their fear of the Parma panthers, they believe that no audience is more satisfying. For this reason, the Regio (like other
European provincial houses) is a proving ground for the young.
Despite everything that has been done to provide opportunities
for beginning singers elsewhere, the provincial opera house is
still the best place to begin.

All provincial theaters are not in the provinces, however.
Among those golden opportunities open to the young are the
training courses and performances of the big Italian management agency in Milan called A.L.C.I. (Associazione Lirica e
Concertistica Italiana), the Sperimentale in Spoleto, and the
Centro di Avviamento of La Fenice in Venice, all open to
young singers from all over the world. These are at provincial
level, offering contracts to trained singers who are ready to
begin their stage careers; but they have the advantage of being
reviewed by big city newspaper critics.

The company underwritten by the A.L.C.I. works in collaboration with the Florentine Association for the Diffusion of
Musical Education with the Cincinnati America Opera Auditions, Inc. This latter association is a nonprofit organization
for the discovery and development of opera talent in America,

and is in direct collaboration with the College conservatory of Music of Cincinnati and with the Taft Enterprises' Radio Cincinnati, Inc. This A.L.C.I. group, one of the most exciting in the business, has put on sixteen consecutive autumn seasons at the modern Teatro Nuovo in Milan—all with young singers who are skimmed from the cream of the international crop. Through this setup the following singers have been heard:

Gigliola Frazzoni	Carlo Bergonzi
Anna Maria Rovere	Adriana Lazzarini
Renata Scotto	Dino Dondi
Giorgio Tozzi	Anselmo Colzani
Pier Miranda Ferraro	Marcella de Osma
Luigi Alva	Anita Cerquetti
Renata Ongaro	Angelo Lo Forese
Otello Bersellini	Giorgio Kokolios
Daniele Barioni	Claudia Parada
Piero Cappuccilli	Gastone Limarilli
Piero Guelfi	Jean Deis
Roald Reitan	Wladimiro Ganzarolli
Bonaldo Giaiotti	Angelo Nosotti
Bruno Prevedi	Prudence Bickus
Rita Orlandi Malaspina	Jeannine Crader
Paolo Montarsolo	Mario Guggia
Orianna Santunioni	Franca Fabbri
Elena Giordano	

Not all of the performances of the Milan organization take place in that city. Whole seasons are organized in cities such as Toulouse in France, Bari and Florence in Italy, and San Sebastián in Spain, giving the winners of these auditions an even wider field in which to make their names known. Proof of the pudding is that the list above includes singers who are now at the top of the international field, as well as singers who are regular, full-time working professionals in lower fee brackets.

The Teatro Lirico Sperimentale of Spoleto is the first and most famous organization of this type. Founded in 1947 by an attorney, Adriano Belli, with the support of Dr. Gaetano Toscano, father of the mayor of Spoleto (one of the most avid supporters of Menotti's Festival of Two Worlds), the Sperimentale opened with a performance of Francesco Ciléa's *L'Arlesiana,* with the composer himself in the audience. From the beginning there have been direct ties with the Rome Opera, a considerable advantage for young singers who have their first big opportunity here. Each January an international competition selects singers who will perform the following September in the Sperimentale season. These winners are given grants which are provided by the Italian government through the Ministry of Tourism and the Ministry of the Theater. After nearly four months of coaching, training, and rehearsing, the Sperimentale goes onstage, presenting a repertory which is chosen according to the capacities of the singers available. The singers who show off to best advantage in the actual performances are put back to study with the same coaches who have prepared them for the Sperimentale. This, too, is made possible by Italian government grants which allow the singer to prepare his entire repertory and get fully ready for a big-time professional debut. The following singers are alumni of the Sperimentale of Spoleto:

Rolando Panerai	Cesare Valletti
Walter Monachesi	Marcella Pobbé
Lucia Danieli	Gian Giacomo Guelfi
Philip Maero	Antonietta Stella
Anita Cerquetti	Franco Corelli
Gabriella Tucci	Umberto Borsò
Orietta Moscucci	Giuseppe Gismondo
Dino Formichini	Lorenzo Testi
Giovanna Fioroni	Giulio Bardi
Margherita Rinaldi	Franco Bonisolli
Mietta Sighele	

Between 1953 and 1958, Fulbright students coming from the United States were also on the Sperimentale roster; and in that group were Anna Moffo, Jimi Beni, Luisa de Sett, William Olvis, Ezio Flagello, and thirty-eight other Americans who made their debuts here.

The Centro di Avviamento of La Fenice in Venice is the only one of these seasons for the young which operates in a major opera house. To the winners of its annual contest—open to men or women under twenty-eight, foreign or Italian, who have perfected their voice technique and are ready for the stage— the Centro offers an intense eight-month course in repertory and *scena*. Ten other young singers, paying their own expenses, are also admitted, after the contest winners are chosen.

The Venice Centro does not teach singing; rather, it expects its applicants to be well above the conservatory graduate level. Here a singer's repertory is built; acting is polished; languages are perfected. Poise comes through prolonged day-to-day contact with major singers from all over the world, for the young professionals of the Centro attend La Fenice rehearsals of full-scale productions and, eventually, sing in them. This course does not lead to "segregated" performances with casts made up entirely of neophytes. Instead, the singers from the Centro are gradually integrated into the regular repertory performances of a theater which is a useful, living component of Venetian daily life—not merely a venerable historic relic. The singers of the Centro are given a patrimony, being taught that a theater is a family, part of that larger family, the city; they learn, sometimes through bitter experience, that a live theater must run big risks, present unknown works, be something more than a museum.

Those who learn at the Venice Centro are not simply given a debut and then set free. The launching of their careers in a stage performance at La Fenice is but the first step in a long, continuing relationship with the company. For a period of three years, the singer is obliged to consult the management of La Fenice about any contracts which are offered him. Thus he is given free management consultations without having to pay agents' fees, but he is under no obligation to accept the counsel given. If he is engaged to sing in an opera at La Fenice and subsequently is offered an engagement at another opera house, he must refuse the outside contract in favor of the home theater. La Fenice, for its part, engages the graduates of its Centro in the regular productions, often for several years, if the singer wishes to continue his ties with the theater which formed him.

This appears to be an altogether satisfactory and professional arrangement, more rewarding to the singer than single-performance debut honors followed by a void. La Fenice has been repaid in solid coin for its efforts. More than 40 per cent of its opera audience and more than 60 per cent of its concert public is made up of young people, reflecting in figures its awareness of young professionals. Rarely indeed does anyone have to suffer a fifty-year-old Mimi or a sixty-year-old "student" Des Grieux at La Fenice.

So successful has the Venice Centro been that one clause of the 1965 law concerning the Italian national opera provides that each theater must establish its own Centro if it is to continue receiving its national subsidy for its regular seasons. It is too much, of course, to hope that all these centers will reach La Fenice' high level of preparation and performance.

Like provincial opportunities, the training seasons described here must be counted on the positive side of the opera ledger, for there is a prevailing high standard, as there is at most provincial opera houses. Indeed, one often feels more certain of seeing a good show at performances staged under these auspices than at some of the larger theaters where aging stars hold the stage for as long as a decade after they should have been retired. At the provincial theater one hears young, fresh voices integrated into a tradition which is often centuries old. Today, provincial is rarely synonymous with "inferior."

CHAPTER

VII

THE REPERTORY AND
THE PUBLIC

The first responsibility of any opera-company management, large or small, is its choice of repertory. Far more important than the selection of singers, conductors, stage directors, and designers is the selection of the opera to be given during a season. For repertory is the very meat of opera, the protein which nourishes everyone in the theater—performers onstage and public out front. Every opera house pays its civic debt in repertory. It entertains, while educating the public and shaping national (or city) taste; it sustains the composer and carries forward a tradition of operatic composition which, until the 1920's, continued unbroken for three centuries. Opera, until our time, was living theater, the arena of day-to-day contact between living composers and a living audience.

Yet in this century, American theaters have come to take their responsibilities less and less seriously. They offer their public only the masterpieces of the past, making it virtually impossible for contemporary composers to gain a hearing.

A glance at the repertories of American professional companies for any season—even the most encouraging—proves at once that the operas given are almost all the works of composers who worked before 1930. Surveying the programs of ten major American opera-producing units, one reads over and over again the names of *Aida, Samson, Tosca, Bohème, Travi-*

ata, Carmen, Butterfly, Rigoletto, Trovatore. Strauss' *Capriccio* is considered a frightful risk; *Gianni Schicchi* and *Wozzeck* "novelties." No one could claim in good faith that these ten companies are living theaters. They are museums, dedicated to the annual exhibition of mummies and sanctified relics. Among all the American professional companies, only Julius Rudel's New York City Opera and the Santa Fe company have the courage to depart regularly from accepted convention.

It is easy to berate the managements of these big companies for their irresponsibility toward living musicians. It is not so easy to account for this terrible lack of balance between the old and the new.

Before examining the situation, let us look at the recent repertories of nine foreign companies with which American companies can be compared:

TEATRO ALLA SCALA, MILAN, ITALY

Cavalleria Rusticana	L'Amico Fritz
Don Carlo	La Fanciulla del West
Il Barbiere di Siviglia	Mefistofele
Katerina Ismailova	La Cenerentola
Il Ritorno di Ulisse in Patria	La Bohème
Lucia di Lammermoor	Elektra
Rise and Fall of the City of	L'Elisir d'Amore
Mahagonny	Miseria e Nobilta
Cardillac	Erwartung
Volo di Notte	Rienzi
Macbeth	Le Nozze di Figaro

TEATRO SAN CARLO, NAPLES, ITALY

L'Africaine	La Forza del Destino
Orfeo	Beatrice Cenci
Lo Sguardo dal Ponte	Katerina Ismailova
Prince Igor	Manon
Carmen	Un Ballo in Maschera
La Figlia di Jorio	Cavalleria Rusticana
Roberto Devereux	Il Barbiere di Siviglia
Die Meistersinger von Nürnberg	

GRAND THÉÂTRE, GENEVA, SWITZERLAND

La Traviata
Le Nozze di Figaro
Der Rosenkavalier
Elektra
Fiery Angel

Fidelio
Samson et Dalila
Manon
Parsifal

TEATRO SÃO CARLOS, LISBON, PORTUGAL

Der Rosenkavalier
Parsifal
L'Heure Espagnole
I Capuleti e i Montecchi
La Traviata
L'Elisir d'Amore

Così fan tutte
Jeanne d'Arc au Bûcher
Carmen
Madame Butterfly
Don Carlo

STAATSTHEATER, STUTTGART, GERMANY

Der Rosenkavalier
La Traviata
The Fairy Queen
Auferstehung
Lucia di Lammermoor
Il Tabarro
Der Wildschütz
Il Turco in Italia
Alceste
Don Giovanni
Così fan tutte
Der Freischutz
Undine
Die Fledermaus
Lohengrin
Tristan und Isolde
Der Ring des Nibelungen
Ariadne auf Naxos
Elektra
La Forza del Destino
Macbeth
Un Ballo in Maschera

Daphne
Otello
Die Legende von der unsicht-
    baren Stadt Kitesch
Gianni Schicchi
Oberon
Jenufa
Jeptha
Die Zauberflöte
Die Entführung aus dem Serail
Fidelio
Die Lustigen Weiber von Wind-
    sor
Zar und Zimmermann
Der Fliegende Holländer
Tannhäuser
Die Meistersinger von Nürnberg
Parsifal
Salome
Capriccio
Il Trovatore
Nabucco
Rigoletto

Aida

Madame Butterfly

Turandot

Don Pasquale

Cavalleria Rusticana

Eugen Onégin

Die Verkaufte Braut

Manon

Les Contes d'Hoffman

Der Mond

Don Perlimplin

Don Carlo

La Bohème

Tosca

Maria Stuart

Il Barbiere di Siviglia

Pagliacci

Boris Godunov

Carmen

Fra Diavolo

Oedipus der Tyrann

Bluthochzeit

NATIONAL THEATER, MANNHEIM, GERMANY

Antigonae (Traetta)

Fidelio

Zar und Zimmermann

Athenerkomödie (Vogt)

The Rake's Progress

Die Entführung aus dem Serail

Die Zauberflöte

Der Fliegende Holländer

Lohengrin

Die Meistersinger von Nürnberg

Parsifal

Il Trovatore

Un Ballo in Maschera

Aida

Falstaff

Daphne

Orfeo ed Euridice

Lucia di Lammermoor

Tosca

Alexandre bis (Martinu)

Die Gärtnerin aus Liebe

Così fan tutte

Ariadne (Handel)

Tannhäuser

Tristan und Isolde

Der Ring des Nibelungen

Rigoletto

La Traviata

Don Carlo

Otello

Boris Godunov

Schwanda

TEATRO COLÓN, BUENOS AIRES, ARGENTINA

Madame Butterfly

L'Heure Espagnole

Simon Boccanegra

Don Rodrigo (Ginastera)

Job (Dallapiccola)

Ernani

Bluebeard's Castle

Lohengrin

Iphigénie en Tauride

L'Enfant et les Sortileges

Norma

Macbeth

Turandot (Busoni)

Oedipus Rex

Le Nozze di Figaro

Ariadne auf Naxos

COVENT GARDEN OPERA, LONDON, ENGLAND

Götterdämmerung	La Bohème
Lohengrin	The Dialogues of the Carmelites
Khovanshchina	Madame Butterfly
Tosca	Macbeth
Rigoletto	Aida
Otello	Falstaff
Don Carlo	Billy Budd
A Midsummer Night's Dream	Fidelio
I Puritani	Manon
Der Rosenkavalier	Katerina Ismailova
Marriage of Figaro	

TEATRO MASSIMO BELLINI, PALERMO, SICILY

La Morte di Rasputin (libretto by Stephen Spender and music by
  Nikolas Nabokov)
Il Barbiere di Siviglia
Samson et Dalila
Vivì (Franco Mannino)
Norma
Madame Butterfly
Il Trovatore
Il Piccolo Marat (Mascagni)

In a glance, one can see how much better balanced the European repertory is than the programs of American professional theaters. European opera houses are required by the national ministries of fine arts to put on new works. If they do not collaborate with living composers, their government subsidies are threatened or withheld. In America, the public is at the mercy of the box office.

Here is what Robert Herman, the artistic administrator of the Metropolitan Opera, has to say about that theater's repertory:

"For new productions, we must, with rare exceptions, choose operas that stand a fair chance of lasting eight to ten years. We cannot afford to send them permanently to the warehouse after five or six performances, as happened with *The Rake's Progress* a few seasons ago, due to lack of public response. We must ration such works, at times braving criticism for being old fashioned. We try to guide public taste, but we do not want to ignore it. Offbeat Verdi (*Nabucco, Ernani*) does better than the very new or the very old. The selfsame Verdi once said that opera houses were meant to be full, not empty. We agree.

"How do we decide what we shall perform? We draw on experience; there is no other way. We own sets for eighty operas, which, if not used, become shopworn just the same. We can afford three or four new productions a season; to refurbish almost the entire repertory has taken fifteen years, and an opera like *The Rake* delayed production of a standard work which might have lasted a decade.

"We advance step by step. First we consult a chart of operas and seasons when performed, which we can survey at a glance. When we see a large, empty space, indicating a too-long absence—as with *The Magic Flute, Falstaff* or *Manon*—that opera gets our first attention. The record readily shows that the Metropolitan was built as an Italian opera house and has remained one, despite several bids for leadership by German works. Even so, we perform in four languages; in making repertory decisions, a balance must constantly be borne in mind.

"We discuss past mistakes, such as a standard opera newly designed early in Mr. Bing's regime but always considered slightly controversial in its production; after a dozen years, we may decide that the time has come for complete restaging. Mr. Bing's opening opera, *Don Carlo,* on the other hand, could hardly be improved upon, so we keep cleaning and mending it. Also, we must choose works which many artists can sing; there is a worldwide dearth of Wagnerian singers and interpreters of French opera. Will we have the right performers for the operas we want, and will they be available two or three weeks to rehearse and perform?

"My second chart, showing the availability of artists, lists names and the weeks of the season. It too is easy to read, once you know how. Red line straight down: unavailable. Blue line: available for performance. Wavy blue line: available for rehearsal. Chart number three concentrates on the daily rehearsal and performance schedules. Pink means piano rehearsals; green, full orchestra; red, an odd subscription series; blue, an even subscription series. Yellow, orange, brown, purple, and green represent series recently added. The color codes of lines, checks, dots and words is the backbone of your season and ours, but with all the new subscriptions, we're in danger of running out of colors.

"We have 14,000 subscribers—our masters. Each of eighteen different subscription series must get a chance to see each new production and each new leading singer as soon as we can arrange it, and we try not to give them the same opera two years in succession. If one essential artist drops out, the entire scheme may have to be redone. Within this framework, the leading singers should get their equitable share of premières and broadcasts. For instance, Birgit Nilsson sang *Aida* on opening night, so Leontyne Price sang it in the season's broadcast. And we try to program the broadcast at least three weeks after the first performance of a new production, so the *Opera News* will have a chance to get photographs for its readers. One of my tools is a high stack of small slips: box office returns for every performance. Some indicate conclusive details, such as the weather on that certain Monday when the tickets went on sale. My colleague, Paul Jaretzki, and I use these slips to double check the wisdom of our recommendations.

". . . Right now, in odd moments, we brainstorm over seasons as much as three years in the future. In April, when we go on tour, Messrs. Bing, Gutman, Schick, Jaretzki and I will consider these at leisure, while in our meeting in hotels, on trains and even beside swimming pools—where, believe it or not, some of our most productive work is done—we still put the final touches on the season to come. Between Labor Day and Easter, the five of us have almost daily planning sessions.

". . . We must ideally have three or four artists available for each major part. We still smart under the memory of February 2, 1963, when in the thick of the flu season, we had 'only' three tenors available for the broadcast matinee of *Der Fliegende Holländer* and had to change the opera, intermission features and all, while part of the audience was already lunching at Sherry's. Years earlier, when Renata Tebaldi fell ill and can-

celled her first Metropolitan *Aida,* Zinka Milanov came to our
rescue by singing her first Metropolitan *Tosca* only a few hours
after we turned to her for help. Last fall, we kept two *Helden-
tenors* here for five performances of *Götterdämmerung,* and
they stood by for each other through the entire German repertory. When Paul Schoeffler fell ill on December 13, Otto
Edelmann's scheduled Hans Sachs was left unprotected. If
Edelmann had developed a cold or sprained an ankle . . .

"To cast some 240 performances a year, down to the last maid
or messenger is no small matter. Our comprimarios are responsible for fifty or sixty slaves, servants, friends, fathers, soldiers,
courtiers or gods. Still, nobody fathoms what could happen in
an opera like *Die Meistersinger,* which requires five leading
and ten secondary singers; practically everyone must be able
to replace someone else, and needs a replacement of his own . . .
We always have one replacement for each role in readiness
within twenty minutes of the Opera House. The alternate conductor, however, is entrusted less to chance; he must be right
in the building, white tie laid out, from thirty minutes before
curtain time until the bitter end . . .

"The term 'planning session' sounds serious. And it is, indeed,
a serious challenge to keep culture entertaining and entertainment cultivated. At a conservative estimate, these sessions take
up to 100 man hours weekly . . .

" 'A general manager does not have to bother with artistic
matters,' Mr. Bing sighed recently. 'All he has to do is read
timetables and worry about the taxes of foreign artists.' "

Because all of these factors come into play when the Metropolitan repertory is being planned, Mr. Bing and his staff have
the toughest managerial job in the opera world. Far, far easier
is the lot of any European *intendant.* The Mannheim director
has his entire roster of singers and conductors on annual salary,
all resident in Mannheim. He does not have to be able to read
timetables, nor does he worry about his artists' tax problems.
His chief task is to plan an imaginative, varied schedule for one
of the most dedicated and sophisticated opera publics on earth.
In the program of the Mannheim season cited earlier in this
chapter, there are *ten* new productions for one year, against the

Metropolitan's four. Hamburg's ultraprofessional Rolf Liebermann, himself a composer of international reputation, is equally
fortunate. Here is a glimpse of what he offered during the two-
week-long International Music Council conference (summer,
1964) at the Staatsoper:

> Krenek's *Le Bouc d'or*
> Henze's *The Prince of Hamburg*
> Britten's *Midsummer Night's Dream*
> Stravinsky's *The Flood*
> Dallapiccola's *The Prisoner*
> Prokofiev's *Love for Three Oranges*
> Orff's *Oedipus der Tyrann*
> Weill's *Rise and Fall of the City of Mahagonny*
> Debussy's *Pelléas et Mélisande*
> Berg's *Lulù* and *Wozzeck*
> Honegger's *Antigone*

Here is what the critic Robert Siohan of *Le Monde* wrote
about the public's reaction:

"It would be presumptuous certainly to pretend that all the
audience was unreservedly enthusiastic about the program
which was offered. Nevertheless, we were able to see that the
theatre, with 1,800 seats, was full for the eight nights we attended."

A manager such as Parma's Negri or La Scala's Ghiringhelli
or La Fenice's Labroca has a slightly more difficult job. He has
to juggle artist's schedules, for he is on the *stagione* system;
but he is in southern Europe, where it is relatively easy to get
a substitute singer within a couple of hours, just by telephoning
to another theater in a nearby city. (The managements of many
American companies, on the other hand, have been forced to
import singers *from Europe* by plane at the last minute to fill
the shoes of an ailing star.)

Like his German counterpart, the Italian general manager is
morally obliged to schedule several new operas or novelties
each season—either works which he premières in his own city
or offers as an Italian or a world première. If he does not do so,
the critics lash him and the government threatens to withdraw

its financial support, cutting down the subsidy because he is not serving modern art along with the "dinosaurs" of the repertory. His problem is exactly the opposite of Mr. Bing's.

Yet Bing shares with all his colleagues in the managerial field—from New York through Europe and all around the world back to New York again—the major problem of the theater: that of pleasing the public. Here, Bing is on firm ground. In his own words: "No one seems to like what we do except the audience."

Another name for audience is that amorphous, generic noun, the public. But what is the public? This is an impossible question to answer. "The public," from the Latin *publicus,* from *poplicus,* from *populus,* which means "the people."

For centuries, the public was a collective term applied to all those men and women who came into the theater and remained there, standing or seated, to watch the performance. How easy it all was then: satisfy the public and have a success. Then the public was visible, even tangible. It could be counted. Its tastes in opera were fairly predictable, for it loved the all-powerful singer and the works which were written for that singer alone. It (like the singer) demanded new works all the time; but this presented no problem, for the great vogue for opera stimulated composers and kept works pouring from their pens. Even the smallest, meanest theater knew its public, and knew that it had to keep putting on new operas in order to sell seats.

True, the public of the seventeenth, eighteenth, and nineteenth century was often difficult. The annals of opera are full of fiascos brought down on the heads of hapless musicians and managers by that capricious devil "the public." Obstreperous, too. Berlioz, visiting Milan, complained that he could not hear the performance at the Teatro Cannobbiana because there was such a clatter of dishes and silverware from the boxholders having supper in their boxes. The public of the San Carlo in Naples was infamous all over Europe for its bad manners. Stendhal had part of his clothes torn off during the elbowing and shoving in the great foyer of that theater. Inside, the audience were "mad as hatters"—"a cage of roaring, ravenous lions, and the doors flung open! Aeolus unleashing the fury of the winds! Nothing can give the least, the sketchiest idea of the rage of a Neapolitan audience insulted by a wrong note." During Rossini's *La Donna del Lago,* the drunks in the pit accompanied the trumpet passages with the noise of troops of galloping horses, produced by beating their walking sticks and leather heels on the floors and seats—small wonder that the benches at the San Carlo had to be replaced every two years! "The whole theatre became a bear-pit," says Stendhal, the audience a roaring horde, all intent on keeping the uproar going. Rossini collapsed and fled. When a minor official of the San Carlo sought him out after the performance and asked the composer to take a curtain bow, Rossini knocked him down with a single blow.

Even on peaceful nights, the noise level in the Italian theater was very high. The gentlemen and nobles moved from box to box as they wished, visiting with friends. Women remained seated, but chatted freely with the occupants of neighboring boxes—even those two or three boxes away! Frequently only the arias were heard. Everything between—orchestra and recitative alike—was drowned out.

For this public of the seventeenth and eighteenth and early nineteenth centuries, opera was something more than entertainment. The theater was their second home, a social gathering place, a hall where everyone could keep warm (and save money by not having to use heat at home) and have a good time. The living room of the city, it served as the corner café serves in Italy and France today. And the stage of yesterday is the café television set of today, while the public has moved from its chairs at the opera house to the chairs which the bar owner ranges around his television set.

The opera theater was once the center of the economic and political life of the city. It was said in Venice that more business was transacted in the *ridotto* of La Fenice than on the Rialto. Families were drawn to the theater almost nightly. It was the rendezvous of everyone.

Musically, these citizens were more *au courant* than the people of today. They knew all the opera scores from memory, because each work was repeated night after night. Decades of listening taught them to weigh the capabilities of various singers against the highest standards known. Thus an informed taste was built up. All this prepared a fertile ground for an unparalleled flowering of the art of music.

But today's public is not yesterday's. No longer is the "public" that group of people sitting in the seats of the theater. It is a faceless, shapeless mass, an international phantom with its ear glued to the speakers of radios, record players, tape recorders; its eye is fixed on television screens and journalists' columns. It was all so simple before the phonograph was invented and when nearly everyone was illiterate. How quickly, for example, opera became the "newspaper" of the day. Old mythological plots quickly gave way to plots drawn from real history, and these could be thinly disguised (because of censorship, disguise was necessary) to cover their direct reference to the intrigues and interests of contemporary life. This "journalistic" opera became the vehicle for political expression and for social satire. Verdi, of course, is the *last* of this line, and not the *first*, as is commonly believed. In our own time, Menotti's *The Consul* speaks with this same voice. If there were more of this kind of opera today, then books such as *The Ugly American, Gone with the Wind, Babbitt, Main Street,* would all be the subjects of operas.

Today's public pays ticket prices on all levels, comes from all walks of life and from all levels of society. But for what reason does it come to the opera? Not just to be entertained, certainly. And not to visit with neighbors in nearby boxes. Many people today, unfortunately, attend opera because it is "the thing to do," but understand little or nothing of what goes on onstage.

In an amusing article in the London *Sunday Times* of August 2, 1964, Frank Giles writes of "A Suggestion for a New Way to Allot Tickets." During a performance of Strauss' *Capriccio* at Glyndebourne, Giles began to ask himself what possible thread existed between the public there and the opera onstage. "What could a Sunday-night gathering of prosperous looking citizens and their wives be getting from this gossamer creation of Strauss and his librettist?

"There were no doubt people in the house that night who had travelled far and spent much to see a masterpiece they either knew or wanted to know. As for the others, it is nobody's business save their own why people should not choose to pay to see and hear words and music whose inner meaning they cannot arrive at.

"All the same, there was something undeniably depressing, as Strauss' magic wove its spell, to see in the row in front a portly, dinner-jacketed figure keel over in honest slumber. Almost as depressing as to hear, in the garden during the interval, an upper-class female voice discussing with friends the characters in the opera: 'She reminds me exactly of Ena Sharples in Coronation Street.' A little farther on, two middle-aged men were reflecting with gusto upon the picnic they had just consumed: 'That bottle of champagne wasn't up to the first at all, old man, not at all. I'm afraid it must have been corked.'

"Sleeping and making homely comments and taking an interest in one's wine are not crimes by any standard. But why go to Glyndebourne to practice them? There is surely a waste of something here, like a colour-blind person going to a Van Gogh exhibition, or serving *tripes à la mode de Caen* to a Buddhist monk, or sending one's aunt to a lecture on aerodynamics. No harm is done, admittedly. But putting square pegs into round holes is always undesirable when it keeps out the genuinely round pegs. And so, at the risk of being called a killjoy and a snob, I propose that applications for Glyndebourne seats should be accompanied by some simple type of aptitude test. The successful candidates would get the seats; those rejected, if really intent on having a musical experience, could try again next year."

The difference between the audience of today and that of one or two centuries ago is that then everybody understood what opera was all about. Today, what a mixed bag! One segment of the public may understand the language which is being sung onstage, while another may interpret the opera solely through the singers' actions. One part of the public may be educated in music, while another holds degrees in science, and yet another has no education at all in opera. One part of the public comes for the music; another part comes to be seen or written about. One group of the contemporary women's guild to save the opera is trying to save it for its music, but another group may be working just to save the opera as a civic monument or a cultural institution. Thus even those who *appear* to care most for opera actually care about something else altogether. In its varied levels of intelligence and perception and appreciation, the public is the most difficult entity in the world.

Add to this hydra-headed monster the people who get in on free passes, the fans, and the claques, and there is an even more complicated beast to please.

"Bravo, Corelli!" screams one fan.

"No!" comes a roar from the other side of the house. "Brava, Stella!"

Rudolf Bing is not by far the only manager to suffer from partisan uproar during the performance. One recalls, not without joy, the havoc wrought at the Metropolitan by the fans of Kurt Baum and Zinka Milanov. At La Scala it was Callas versus Tebaldi. More lately, Stella versus Corelli. There is nothing new here. The celebrated rivalry of Cuzzoni and Bordoni kept London boiling for years; but one suspects that even those two artists would have had to give way to Grace Moore and Jan Kiepura on the feuding ground.

The claque is also part of the public, holding its own in spite of managerial attacks. Paid applause has been part of theatrical tradition since Greek times, and it reappears in the theater of Plautus' time in Rome. Tacitus even cites one chief claquer by name. It is said that Nero's claque numbered five thousand men, a figure to make some of our contemporary Italian tenors blanch with envy. Even the actors of medieval mystery plays were greeted with paid applause; and it is through this channel that the tradition passed to the Italian stage and to the opera. It came to be regarded as a Venetian vice. Some impresarios were forced to support a claque in order to obtain a lease for a given theater. In Bologna, at the Teatro Formagliari in 1761, we have the first recorded instance of a theater director refusing to let the claque into the house, but the claquers got in anyway (as they always do, even at La Scala and at the Met, though both theaters have mounted a ten-year offensive against them), and for pure vengeance created such an uproar in the theater that the opera was forced to close. The next night the claque was admitted. Heavy with gratitude, they applauded the opera until it was declared an unqualified success.

The power of the claque is great. In Rome in the last decades of the eighteenth century, the head of the claque was even consulted by the management on the choice of operas to be programed. At La Scala, the master claquer Fossati became so expert that he could control the whole public with a handful of men, using just a flick of the hand or a twitch of his eyebrow for his signals. Fossati had two regular "seasons," just like an artist. He spent his winters in Milan and the summers at the Teatro Colón of Buenos Aires. Of more recent memory is a Metropolitan Opera claquer who disrupted the first act of an opera at the Mosque Theatre in Newark, New Jersey, on an evening when the baritone—one of the best singers of his generation—refused to pay a claque and was nearly booed off the stage as a result. The second act went better because he paid off the claque during the intermission.

Today the claque is held awkward, obvious, and embarrassing by the managements of all the big theaters of the opera trade. Unfortunately, many of the most prominent singers feel that they need the support of the hirelings in order to get through a performance successfully. And although the managements of houses such as the Met and La Scala and San Francisco, and even London and Paris, do everything in their power to discourage them, the claquers survive. The theater tries to exert gentle pressure on the singers: "Now, look here, you don't need that kind of applause." The managements try to point out that a claque frequently does as much harm as good. More direct action can be taken at the box office, where recognized claquers or their henchmen are refused tickets. But oh, the wiles used by these crafty gentlemen once they are armed with a singer's money. Once, they bought blocks of tickets outright. Now they are adept at scattering in pairs through the upper reaches of the theater, and sometimes several of them are planted in expensive orchestra seats. In some American opera houses (civic companies, of course, and not workshops), the libretto sellers are the claquers, just as they were in Venice three hundred years ago.

Most American claquers are from southern Italy—that is, from Naples and points beyond. But in Paris, just as in the last century, they are chiefly Romans and are called *Romains,* not *claqueurs.* Every one of these experts had his own title and set of qualifications. Some were "encore-masters"; some were "weepers," who cried during the tragic scenes and induced the rest of the public to cry; some were "connoisseurs," who were self-declared masters of technique and only shouted with joy when a singer executed an unusually difficult passage. There was even a graduated pay scale (which still applies in some modern theaters) with simple applause paid at a given figure, a double salvo of applause at a higher rate, and so on, covering single curtain calls, unlimited calls, sighs, howls of joy. In Parma, it is claimed that this graduated scale was evolved by the master claquer of the Regio, who was so powerful in the city that he was called Count Ludovico of Parma.

The average claquer in Italy today is paid about ten dollars per night. Fees for student claquers are two-fifty plus a seat. Top claquers get a seat and sixteen dollars per night. American fees run slightly higher. At certain concerts by opera stars, as many as 150 claquers are planted in the hall. It is rumored that the recent American debut of a European pop idol cost his entrepreneurs more than fifteen thousand dollars for claquers' fees and tickets. For better or worse, no opera star in the world could afford such extravagance. Two or three hundred dollars per night is very nearly top money for the claque. And if managers ever get their way, singers will be spared even that sum.

At the moment, it seems that custom (and not management) will put the claque out of business, for the claque exists only where demonstrations in the theater are loud and noisy. Today, heaven help us, the opera house has become more respectable than a D.A.R. tea. "Whistles at the theater are out of date," blares an Italian headline (*Il Gazzettino di Venezia,* March 5, 1964). "We are all becoming gentlemen." The audience sits through opera in religious silence. At the proper places they applaud—with or without the assistance of the claque. When the performance is fair or poor, they sit on their hands and greet the singers with chilly silence or a polite patter of clapping. But where are the whistles, the shrieks, the yells, the boos, the howls of outraged ticket-holders? Silence has fallen on a once-noisy scene.

Time was when the third act was the terror of every theatrical performer. Let the show drag a bit, let it run a little long, let the public get away for a second—and the evening was lost. First, there would be restlessness and an occasional "Sssshhh," forewarning of disaster, followed by the full-blown demonstration. In some theaters the public even threw its chairs on the stage (either up from the pit or down from the boxes) as a sign of disapproval; and we do not have to go back to the Jockey Club's disruption of Wagner's *Tannhäuser* to find an example of an organized demonstration in the opera house. Menotti's *The Consul* was whistled (literally, with children's toy whistles) from the La Scala stage; and Luigi Nono's *Intolleranza 1960* sparked a major political riot which brought the police into La Fenice and emptied the theater during the performance. The noisiest demonstration of very recent years took place at Covent Garden at the première of Sam Wanamaker's new production of *La Forza del Destino*, but it appears to have been spontaneous and not preorganized. The point at hand, though, is that it is extremely rare today to hear a big demonstration in the opera house.

A king-sized scandal resulted from a sound whistling which the Parma public delivered to an unfortunate cast in 1962. Attacked in a Milanese newspaper as "clowns, filled with ridiculous presumption, a public which stinks of pride, of delinquency, and of bad manners," the people of Parma responded to defend their rights.

Their case ran something like this: "The singers were rotten, not up to the tasks assigned them. The singers knew this before the performance started. The management knew it. If the performance is good, we applaud, shout, cry, we are unreservedly generous with our praise. But if the performance is poor, should we clap? No. We remember great performances, and not just 'golden age' performances, but those of Tebaldi,

Carlo Bergonzi, Flaviano Labò, and other recent singers. We would be disloyal to these great singers and to ourselves if we applauded the rubbish which we heard onstage the other night. We would be doing the singers themselves a great disservice, for we would be deceiving them and encouraging them to go on singing badly. Far better to whistle, and let them know how bad they are. Also to let the management know that there is still at least one public left on earth which will not tolerate such inferior music. And anyway, we paid good money to get into the theater. Nobody gave us a free ticket. And so we have every right on earth to demonstrate however we like. We are not clowns, nor are we delinquents. But we know our music, and nobody is going to cheat us."

The Parma public will not tolerate mediocrity. But how different other theaters are! Even at the biggest and most expensive opera houses one hears performances which can be compared unfavorably to operas given by *stagione* companies in cities as small as Utica, New York, or Springfield, Massachusetts, twenty years ago. Yet no one protests. Bad as some of these shows are, there is always that patter of genteel applause.

Some critics attribute the new politeness to a general high tone which pervades all middle-class society. The bourgeoisie have always been notoriously afraid of getting out of step, of making spectacles of themselves. The conformism of the decade of the sixties is international: Italy, Australia, New York, Hawaii, Germany, everywhere the same. Everyone behaves himself. No one forgets to toe the line.

On the other hand, there is a school of critics who think that the whole attitude of the theatergoing public has changed. The public once went to *challenge* singers to be as good as they were said to be, to *prove* that they were worth the fees paid to them. Now, no one cares. The attitude in the theater is that of the man who is at home in front of his television set. He listens, but he is not prepared to respond. Just as at the movies no one cheers any more, so also at the opera house. Rarely do people whisper or cough in the theater. Anyone who talks *sotto voce* to another member of the audience is almost blackballed on the spot.

An Italian writer points out that there is something wrong somewhere: when the tempo of life was relatively calm outside the theater, the public exploded in the theater. Now that the tempo of life outside the theater is frenetic and wild, the theater has become a mausoleum. Is it indifference? Perhaps it is simply the fact that life itself is so filled with crises that the crises of the opera stage seem hollow and pallid.

Whatever the reason, whistles and boos have gone out of style in most opera houses. The singer no longer needs fear ripe tomatoes thrown from the balcony. During the rowdiest Italian theatrical demonstration of this decade, the most dangerous missile hurled was a roll of toilet paper; and not even an eyelash flickered at its arrival onstage. It was removed by one of the singers as if it had been a bouquet of roses.

The audience today is so cool that on taped broadcasts of operas (whether from London, from New York, or from Milan) the applause frequently has to be filled in or artifically supplemented. "It really *is* the devil when we have to insert the claque on Ampex!" exclaimed the director of one of Radio Italiana's provincial plants. He is in his late sixties, and he remembers when the audience tore the theater apart—either with enthusiasm or with rage. Those were better days, he sighs.

If anyone doubts that the attitude of today's public is different from the public of, say, Caruso's day or earlier, let him listen to the IRCC (International Record Collectors' Club) disc of Melba's *Les Huguenots* from the Met, recorded by Colonel James Mapleson on wax cylinders in the offstage wings of the house. To say that the public goes wild is to understate the case. The recording of the demonstration and uproar which follow Melba's last notes are almost more valuable as a historic document than the recording of Melba's voice.

A cool public produces a cool singer. Or does a cool singer produce a cool public?

No one knows the answer to that question. But once there was fire on stage (as witness that Melba record, or Caruso's recordings, or Schipa's, or Aureliano Pertile's or Frances Alda's or Francesco Tamagno's or Martinelli's) and now there is a long, well-bred procession of somnolent Violettas and Lucias, of neat, college-grad Alfredos, of icy Leonoras. Any singer who turns on what Gigli used to call "the juice" is accused of vulgarity, of bad taste, and is assailed in the press as a poor musician, a "violator" of the scores, perverter of the composer's wishes.

Once the public wept (with or without the prodding of the claque's "criers"), and now no one sheds a tear. The theater is a house of vivid memories. Even within this century, people cried at Farrar's Butterfly, at Albanese's Traviata, at Bori's Manon, at the *Bohème* fourth act as sung by Charles Kullman, Norina Greco, and Virgilio Lazzari. As late as the nineteen-fifties, the public wept in the opera house. But the sixties have gone cold.

Everybody is a loser: nobody wins. The singer is less excited at the prospect of singing. You have to look to Carol Channing or Louis Armstrong to get that electric shock which used to come from opera, to find a performer not afraid to make a spectacle of himself onstage. The audience responds in kind: it is less ready to participate. The manager is denied even that elementary satisfaction of knowing that, for better or worse, he has touched people's hearts.

"Well, what did they think of it?" the artistic director of a big, modern opera house was asked as he sat in a restaurant after a world première.

"I'll be damned if I know," came the answer. "We'll have to read the papers tomorrow to find out."

CHAPTER

VIII

PIT AND STAGE

The wheel of fortune turns. Twenty-five years ago the fickle goddess smiled on the conductor; before that, on the composer; and before that, on the singer. The man of the current decade in opera is the director, *le regisseur, il regista,* the new god whose spectacular and unprecedented rise cannot be compared to any operatic phenomenon since the triumph of stars over composers in the baroque era.

The post-1950 period is the director's alone. It is the time of Luchino Visconti's *Traviata,* Giorgio De Lullo's *Trovatore,* Margaret Webster's *Aida,* Giorgio Strehler's *Mahagonny,* Louis Malle's *Rosenkavalier,* Jean-Louis Varrault's *Wozzeck,* Jean Vilar's *Macbeth,* Sam Wanamaker's *La Forza del Destino,* Wieland Wagner's *Tannhäuser,* Franco Zeffirelli's *Falstaff,* Günther Rennert's *Il Barbiere di Siviglia.*

But where is the composer's name? Ah, yes, there it is, in small print, down at the bottom of the poster. Or perhaps it is not there at all. Who cares about the composer, after all, when a big-name director is on hand to tell us how the opera should be performed? Just let the director lay his hands on the score, and a whole new work shall be born; for we are living witnesses to an *aggiornamento* and renewal both ecclesiastical and theatrical.

This major shift in emphasis has not been effected overnight, although the director often appears to have been born only yesterday. As the singer relinquished his power, as it was wrested from him, other members of the theatrical complex pushed in to seize what they could from the singer's treasure. First the composer seized the reins; then, after the death of Puccini, we entered into the full-blown era of the conductor; and this, in turn, has given way to the rule of the director.

The entire seizure has been accomplished since roughly the beginning of the Industrial Revolution—which brings to light a strange paradox. During the very period which marked the separation of the idea of usefulness from the ideas of art and beauty, during the period which saw the definition of art as something useless, extraneous, and without practical value, during the period when the words "practical" and "convenient" became measuring sticks for what man must have, three of the most pedestrian operatic crafts became "art." They are, of course, orchestral time-beating, scenic design, and stage direction. Formerly purely mechanical operations, they suddenly flowered as creative acts and interpretive functions.

The forerunners of the modern conductor were the *maestro al cèmbalo*, who was the harpsichordist, and the *maestro concertatore*, who was sometimes—but not always—the first violinist; they handled the chores which fall to the conductor today. The former kept the orchestra in tempo, regulating the beat. The latter supervised rehearsals, pulled together the vocal elements (chorus and soloists) and kept them abreast of the orchestra. The *maestro concertatore* was the equivalent of the modern rehearsal supervisor or assistant conductor, and he was sometimes the *maestro al cèmbalo* as well. Verdi's first chance to make his name known in Milan came in 1834, when he accepted an invitation to "put together" (*concertare*) a performance of Haydn's *The Creation* at the Teatro dei Filodrammatici.

The *maestro concertatore* and the *maestro al cèmbalo* were almost always anonymous, for attention was focused on the composer, who prepared his works for the stage, both at the world première and at various premières in national and provincial capitals. On the playbill for the world première of *La*

Traviata, for example, the Teatro La Fenice listed the names of the composer, librettist, singers, music publisher, scenic designer, choreographer, ballet soloists and minor dancer, but no conductor. And this was as late as 1853, in a city as large as Venice.

The first conductor of opera, had, however, already been launched in Italy some eight years before. Angelo Mariani was born in Ravenna on October 12, 1824. Thus he was Verdi's junior by eleven years, almost exactly to the day. Mariani commenced his musical career as bandmaster, but soon he was violinist and violist at Macerata and Rimini. By 1844 he had advanced to the post of *maestro concertatore* of an opera season in Trent. Autumn and Carnival seasons of that same year found Mariani in Messina, where he was *maestro concertatore* and first violinist, conducting the orchestra (when necessary) with his violin bow as he sat in his chair, according to the custom of the time.

It was in Milan that Mariani's true career began, in Milan that he became an opera conductor. He made his Milanese debut at the Teatro Re with Verdi's *I Due Foscari* in 1846, but Verdi himself was not in the theater that night. Verdi's pupil, Emanuele Muzio, describes this performance as "perfect," though he makes no direct reference to Mariani, who was *maestro concertatore* and first violinist. Again, from Muzio, we learn that *I Lombardi alla Prima Crociata*—given at the Teatro Carcano on August 23, 1846—was sensationally successful, "but the singers are without merit." Here Mariani created an uproar night after night with his expert playing of the violin solo from this opera. "The theater was packed as early as six in the evening," wrote Muzio. From this and other accounts of these performances of *Lombardi,* it is evident that the weight of the performance was borne by Mariani. The following year, 1847, at the Carcano, Mariani was the conductor of *Nabucco,* which he performed with such fire and patriotic fervor that he was threatened with arrest and imprisonment by the Austrian police charged with keeping order in "ungovernable Milan."

From even this brief glance at Mariani's life, one can trace the first steps of Toscanini's predecessor, taken in a turbulent period and pushed forward with the thrust of Verdi's best patriotic music and the impetus of the Italian liberation.

In previous periods, a conductor was not necessary to opera. The first orchestras were but a handful of instruments, played by hardened professionals who would have been insulted had one of their number stood up with a baton and told them what to do. Their performances, like those of a chamber ensemble, were almost self-propelled—the result of long, careful rehearsals. The opening beat and any additional necessary guidance were provided by the first violin.

All this was made possible, of course, because the small orchestras of the time were easily regulated. Monteverdi wrote for thirty-nine instruments. And here is the growth during the eighteenth century of the opera orchestra of the Teatro San Carlo of Naples:

> 1737—45 instruments
> 1740—50 instruments
> 1742—55 instruments

and of La Scala:

> 1770—56 instruments
> 1778—67 instruments

The Paris Opera in the years between 1830 and 1878 had an orchestra which numbered around seventy-five members; but Wagner's instrumentations required 110 instruments—about four times the number which had played in the Venetian opera theaters of the seventeenth century. We know, for example, that the Teatro San Giovanni Crisostomo (now the Malibran) in Venice had an orchestra of forty men at the height of the public opera-house vogue of the late 1600's. (The Metropolitan presently counts 135 orchestra members.) The conductor was not needed for another century and a half.

A direct descendant of Angelo Mariani was Toscanini, who, like Verdi and Mariani, was a native of the physically and culturally rich Emilia-Romagna provinces. Between the two men came a host of famous operatic conductors: Franco Faccio, Edoardo Mascheroni, Giovanni Bottesini. But it is astonishing

to think how close Toscanini was to the very fountainhead of
operatic conducting. Mariani died in 1873; Toscanini was born
in Parma in 1867.

The role of the modern conductor is that of *maestro,* which
is to say "master." He orders. He commands. Others obey. He
conveys the scores to the musicians and to the public. Odd it
is that two hundred years ago—or even one hundred years ago—
when the operatic repertory was a growing thing, a constantly
renewed chain of fresh scores (like the New York musical-
comedy stage), there was no need for a conductor. Each composer was able to clarify his own scores. Very few revivals were
given, for the public did not want "revived" *Don Giovanni.* It
wanted new *Trovatore,* new *Faust,* new *Huguenots.* Now that
the repertory has become a collection of museum pieces, one of
the chief tasks of the conductor is to "interpret" the scores of
dead composers for a living public. Thus he occupies a key
position as translator, yet he is not a creator.

The era of the conductor has lasted roughly for a hundred
and fifteen years; but the era of the Mariani personality lasted
only until the death of Toscanini, until the retirement of Victor
de Sabata. True, Tullio Serafin was still active in Verona in
1963, where he conducted his fiftieth anniversary performance
at the Arena. Nor can the genius of Gianandrea Gavazzeni and
Carlo Maria Giulini be denied; they, too, are directly in the
Toscanini tradition.

But on the whole, impassioned conducting is an outgrowth
of musical romanticism which is not likely to survive in a
mechanized age. An epoch in which people are numbers—auto-
mobile license numbers, social security numbers, postal zone
numbers, armed forces numbers—needs an IBM machine, not a
conductor. A timekeeper can handle the job nicely, nor is Di
Stefano's allusion to the "icebergs" again out of order. Too
often there seems to be a wall of glass between the conductor
and the music.

For Toscanini, on the other hand, music was reality. Music
was life itself. In the contemporary conductor, as in many
young musicians, one senses a detachment, if not indeed a
separation, from music. Like the singer of today, the conductor

would be embarrassed by an excess of emotion. Let no one misunderstand this: Toscanini permitted no nonsense from his singers, no violation of the music. But he lived the music. So also did Serafin and De Sabata and others of their period. Living it, they made the music itself live and brought its composer to life.

No better anecdotes than the following illustrate Toscanini's sense of identification with the composer: Once, during a rehearsal, an orchestra player asked Toscanini if he wanted a crescendo on a certain note. "Brahms wants it, not Toscanini," came the Maestro's reply. And on another occasion, when the orchestra played perfectly: "Play it again. It makes me so happy I could die."

Toscanini was remote from the obsessions of star-egoism. The Toscaninis of the past kept the Melbas in line, even though conductors were mistrusted in turn by composers who thought they held too much interpretative power. Today the entire musical ensemble is under control, with the notable exception of the clutch of Italian tenors. Good manners, not temperament, is the rule of the stage. And even good manners are forgotten when the conductor is too abstracted from his music. One remembers vividly a celebrated German conductor who once kept up a long conversation with friends in the first row at the Metropolitan while he conducted *Don Giovanni*. A metronome could have done his job.

The role of the conductor is to regulate a huge orchestra, only one instrument of which is the human voice. No longer does the conductor agonize with the music, grind his teeth and shout "*Dài! Dài!*" ("Give!"). He is chiefly concerned with balance, like a sound engineer; with tone and power, and with using the entire orchestra as his own instrument. The modern conductor snorts with scorn at colleagues who pamper the singer excessively. The singer exists merely to serve him.

It was said of Furtwängler that he was like "a priest who officiated at a sacred rite," rather than a conductor. His solemn look, his abstraction from "work," his orchestra—which emanated a sweet mystical sound—all contributed to this effect. With Furtwängler, the audience "had to make the brain work, rather than abandon itself to emotion." He dramatized sound, reducing it to pure essence. Toscanini, on the other hand, produced a sound which was the projection of his own soul and a re-creation of the composer's. He was concerned, indeed, with *la musica,* not with sound. Yet Furtwängler's style is much closer to what modern man—the cool generation—seeks, much more satisfying to modern need. Metronome conductors of the present day are well on the road back to the method of the time beaters of the eighteenth century, so remote are they from the music they conduct.

Paul Valéry called the profession of orchestral conductor *véritablement sacre* (truly holy), and it may be that we have finally arrived at the point where conductors think of themselves in this way. Like Furtwängler, they are all priests whose congregations may participate aesthetically but not emotionally. The public may be transported, but let it not laugh or cry. For few conductors now plunge themselves voluptuously into the music, nor do they allow singers to do so. No one may forget himself, and no one may be carried away. These are the new rules of the game. Fortunately, not all conductors observe them.

Since the conductor is the master of the whole opera ensemble, he merits the respect of all. The only man in the complex who knows every single musical and dramatic element of the performance, he could, ideally, act as stage director and plot the action from what he knows about the score.

The first contemporary directors to attempt this were Herbert von Karajan and Thomas Schippers. Curiously, they are at opposite poles as conductors, the former being a "priest" of the Furtwängler breed, the latter much more emotional and involved, more a conductor of the Toscanini-Serafin genre than most of his colleagues. Serving as both orchestral conductors and stage directors, they have projected themselves and their vocation into a new dimension and have perhaps lighted the way toward a whole new concept in opera.

Theoretically, there is no one better equipped to shape the stage action than the conductor himself. Since many conductors begin their careers as voice teachers, coaches, chorus masters, instrumentalists, composers, or even singers, they may know a whole repertory of operas both musically and scenically, long before they have a chance to take the baton in hand and mount the podium. Conductors, by tradition far more intelligent than the average operatic musician, vocal or instrumental, are intellectually equipped to undertake the *régie* of an operatic production.

But as Schippers points out, directing is a very specialized job—demanding, because the modern public at every level in every country knows through films what good direction is. "Great *régie* is a matter of real creation," says Schippers. "We can't expect everyone to be able to do the job really well. Remember that the conductor often doesn't care about the drama. He ought to, but he doesn't. What about that? If conductors were better 'dramaticians' we would be set." Schippers adds that a strong conductor can defend himself, the composer, and the opera against a capricious director, but a weak conductor accepts the ridiculous innovations and *gaucheries* of the sensation seekers.

"Blame conductors a little bit for the take-over of the director. If more conductors had guts, the director would never have been able to take over opera." Schippers is modest enough about his own first steps in the director's world, generous enough toward many of the directors with whom he has worked. A good *regista*, he says, admits that he needs the counsel of the conductor. But many directors, inflated with conceit, tend to take over the opera completely and reshape it to suit their own whims and personal tastes. A conductor-director is much less likely to do this, having a basic respect for the score and a profound understanding of it, as well as a knowledge of the opera's traditional setting.

Conductors, inspired to new vigor of action by the fresh initiative of Karajan and Schippers, may enter the directorial field, thus setting to rights many of the current abuses opera suffers. But much courage is demanded of the man who dares to confront the director, the lion of the modern stage.

"I'm going to open a school for directors where only one subject will be taught: humility," declares Mario Labroca,

former administrator of La Scala and present artistic director
of La Fenice in Venice. But one's immediate response is: it is
too late. To override the arrogance of the modern director is
no easy task. "To direct (*mettre en scène*) means 'interpret' to
me," Wieland Wagner is quoted as saying in Walter Panofsky's
biographical study. But what is the real role of the director?
Ought he to interpret? Why?

Like the conductor, the *director* is a relatively new phenomenon in opera, although the *stage director* is as old as opera
itself. From the earliest Greek theater, from the moment one
actor (usually the chief comedian) gave orders to the rest of
the company, there has been some kind of stage direction in
the theater. Sometimes one of the singers in opera—often the
capocomico, as in Greek theater—sometimes the composer himself, sometimes the impresario, sometimes the *maestro concertatore* had to handle the job; but none of these men ever
thought of assigning himself any special title or assigning his
function an air of importance.

The man whom we know as the "stage director" came into
the opera picture during the last century as the chief stage
mechanic, a backstage jack-of-all-trades who saw that the
scenery was in place; that an adequate crew of stagehands was
in the theater; that the curtain went up on time; that everyone
got onstage and offstage on cue; that all the props were in
place; that the stage effects worked—the moon and the sun
rose or set at the right points in the score, the lighting functioned as planned; that all doors opened and closed, to save
the singers embarrassment; that no member of the cast was
tippling too heavily in his dressing room.

This stage director, often born into a theatrical family such
as the Agninis of San Francisco or the Stivanellos of New York,
virtually lives in the opera house, often spending up to eighteen
hours a day there, traveling from one engagement to another,
sometimes bringing costumes and scenery and props with him,
coaching singers in stage deportment, and generally setting the
tone of the performance. His importance in opera cannot be
overstated, though he works in the shadows, never designating
himself as an artist. The Agninis served San Francisco for
decades; Stivanello, the son of a dramatic soprano and a Vene-

tian costumer, figures heavily in the management of a dozen-odd companies, having lived in an opera world almost from birth.

These men, and those few like them left in the field of stage direction, know opera scores and librettos from end to end. If a singer misses a cue, the stage director is behind the curtain ready to save the situation, giving the lost phrase in half-voice, so the performer can hear and the audience, hopefully, cannot. When something goes wrong with the performance a groan and a curse go up backstage from the stage director, who has heard the second violin come in two bars early or the horns miss an attack in the overture. Nothing in the performance escapes him, for the stage director has at his fingertips the world of opera in all its staggering detail—a repertory of more than a hundred works, sung by more than a thousand singers. Opera is his whole existence; he has no social life, no private life. He is the workhorse of traditional opera, a highly paid expert who is often so busy in the theater that he has no time to spend what he earns.

Very different indeed is the life of today's "director," who lets it be known at once that he is an artist, not a stage mechanic. He is a social butterfly, always to be found at press cocktail parties, after-theater suppers. He "interprets" the opera, "creates" singers, whom he coaches in acting. Often he designs the settings and costumes as well, though he sometimes tows his own chosen benjamin, a designer, in his wake. The director is now so completely master of the modern stage that he may wreak all kinds of havoc with an opera score without hearing a protest from either composer (if he is alive) or management. But how came this ascendancy, and when? Like publicity, another new "art" of the theater, both stage design and stage direction came into view during the last century. An Italian critic of 1901 wrote, not without bitterness, of the rise to power of these operatic elements between 1840 and 1900:

"Cliques and collaborations are shaped, names are manu-factured, under the titles of 'art' and 'artist,' but always to the immense advantage of speculators and those in search of notoriety.

"Oh, the beautiful simplicity of the old-time public which asked only the names of the composer and the singers! They cared nothing about the costumer, less still about the costume designer. What did it matter that the stage revolved, or that the designs were drawn from original paintings in the British Museum or the Bibliothéque Nationale of Paris? They enjoyed the delights of the music alone. Oh, sweet, dear simplicity!

"The composer wrote what his temperament ordered him to write, and the public applauded what it liked. This was the sum and total of the theatrical experience. Everything else was of no importance at all: no one talked of 'the production' before; people judged the opera *after* having heard it. The composer, the singers and the public were more ingenuous, more sincere.

"Then each theatre had one castle, one garden and one prison to serve as sets for an entire repertory—always the same, always the same portraits—the same ancestors in costumes of no period whatsoever, good for all historical epochs and all countries. In the garden, always the same paper flowers, the same brick-colored roses, flowering eternally on the curtains painted by a hack whose name we never learned . . . and always the skinny rocks of cardboard and wood which never tried to conceal their humble origins. These settings never sent any impresario into bankruptcy.

"But now, just think that there are composers who are more concerned with the scenic and decorative minutiae than with the music! And think that a modern theatrical management often thinks first of the setting and second of the choice of singers."

This in the year 1901. The essay comes from an Italian commemorative publication issued at Verdi's death.

Sixty-five years later, opera is merely another tool of those who manipulate setting, action, and décor. Whether they have swallowed opera or saved it from oblivion is a moot question. For if in motion pictures the director is the only true father of the art, the same certainly cannot be said of opera. The composer is the father of the music, and music too often comes last in the modern opera theater.

Though an emerging force in the last century, the director truly came into his operatic kingdom after World War II, when the powerful, realistic *régie* of Rossellini and Fellini in films made the often stylized acting of operatic singers seem inadequate to the new needs of the European continental public.

The two foremost directors were Luchino Visconti and Wieland Wagner, the former working south of the Alps, the other at Bayreuth. Both men were heirs to an immensely rich family tradition in general culture, in art, music, literature, and theater.

Visconti is defined in the *Enciclopedia dello Spettacolo* as *"regista e scenarista cinematografico, librettista e regista di balletto."* The word "opera" is only implied; and we see at once how far we have come since the decades when Verdi and Wagner supervised the productions of their own works.

Yet Visconti has a certain tie with opera through his family's interest, generations old, in La Scala; he is a musician, having studied cello in his childhood and youth. His technical career began in France, under Jean Renoir, but he shifted at once back to native soil and worked as a director in Milan. Emerging also as a writer and critic, Visconti set forth his ideas for a complete renewal of the Italian cinema, which he wished to re-create as a national, popular, realistic art. His sole hope at that time was that Italy might play a significant role in European theater.

It was Visconti who brought Jean-Paul Sartre, Tennessee Williams, Arthur Miller, Ernest Hemingway, Erskine Caldwell, Jean Cocteau and Jean Anouilh to the Italian public at the Teatro Eliseo in Rome; Visconti who gave Italy exacting, re-studied productions of dramas by Carlo Goldoni, Anton Chekhov, August Strindberg, Pierre Augustin Beaumarchais, and Euripides; Visconti who dared an electrifying *Crime and Punishment* and a rococo *As You Like It* with Dali scenery and costumes.

When he finally laid his hands on opera, Visconti had a certain respect for the art, but he was not afraid of it. Wanting it modern, wanting it spectacular, he set in motion in Milan a chain of cause and effect which has yet to be broken.

Visconti's first opera was Gasparo Spontini's *La Vestale* at
La Scala in 1954, to be followed shortly by *La Sonnambula*
and *La Traviata* in 1955, *Anna Bolena* in 1957, and Gluck's
Iphigénie en Aulide in 1957. Outside of Milan, he staged *Don
Carlo* for Covent Garden; *Macbeth* for the inaugural of the
Spoleto Festival; and Donizetti's *Il Duca d'Alba* and Strauss'
Salome for Spoleto in 1959 and 1961, respectively. These are
but a handful of his many, sometimes successful, nearly always
sensational productions.

Because Maria Callas was often the leading soprano of Visconti's productions, a certain amount of her notoriety rubbed
off on Visconti. But he had little real need of a "personality" to
draw attention to his works. Like Wieland Wagner, Visconti
was his own publicity mill. And, like Wagner, he often used
sensation and shock to catch the eye of press and public. Let it
be understood that a director often needs shock tactics to catch
the eye of the public; for while a good conductor can evoke
the comment "It was a revelation" from an admiring audience
without violating the score, a director has a hard time creating
a "sensation" without making major changes.

As Visconti worked in Italy, Wieland Wagner, eleven years
his junior, was "re-creating" his grandfather's works at Bayreuth.
There, at least, was a father-son tradition; yet a comparison of
the productions of Wieland with those of his brother Wolfgang
makes it amply clear that it was Wieland who, like Visconti,
was bent on sweeping reforms which would purge opera of
many of its conventional elements.

The first echoes of Wieland Wagner's productions to reach
the outside world brought news of Valkyrs without helmets, of
a *Ring* without a dragon, of singers teetering precariously on a
raked stage, groping in the dark for cues and for other members
of the cast.

Building on foundations laid by Adolphe Appia, Wieland
Wagner stripped the stage of every nonessential element. While
Visconti was draping *Traviata* with velvets and fringes of the
1880's, Wagner was laying bare the most basic dramatic elements
of his grandfather's work. It is abundantly clear that while both
were aiming at a complete housecleaning, they were following

radically different paths. Yet both men—one drastically scraping opera, the other smothering it—ignored to a shocking degree the composer's explicit directions for staging, running rough-shod over tradition and the original libretto to achieve their own new operatic colors and tones. In short, both men are the "creators" whom Verdi profoundly mistrusted, the reshapers and cutters whom Wagner would have sent straight into Fafner's hole. Many of the directors who have followed these two masters lack both the taste and the intelligence of Visconti and Wagner, to say nothing of their general culture. Out of the void of ignorance have come many horrors of the modern operatic stage, operas which the original composers would not recognize as their own.

Opera-house managements, seeing that big-name directors often attract the audience more readily than a leading singer, engage men from the legitimate stage and from films—even though many of these operatic parvenus do not know opera, possibly have never even seen an operatic performance, have little interest in opera, and do not know music.

"This is my first encounter with opera," said Jean-Louis Barrault, interviewed at the Paris Opéra just at the outset of the *Wozzeck* rehearsals. And arriving at the Metropolitan to stage *Faust,* he added, "I know nothing about the technical nature of music."

"I don't know anything about music, and don't intend to learn," Louis Malle stated, shortly after his arrival in Spoleto, where he directed a new production of *Rosenkavalier.*

"My interest in opera was born and died in the early 1930's at the Chicago Opera House," said Sam Wanamaker, who admits that he is not a musician, that he learned *La Forza del Destino* from listening to commercial recordings.

Yet directors of this caliber are not above pontificating about opera. Without modesty they boast of "interpreting the operas of the past" for today's audience, of "illuminating" scores for singers and conductors. Such arrogance has bred disasters without number.

It is clear, of course, that not all directors are uniformly ignorant about the art which they are so eager to overhaul.

When the director knows opera profoundly, when he understands the composer, the librettist, the score, and the drama, when he wishes to cast new light on the work and not simply turn out a spectacle, the results are often exciting. The genius of a great director ought to be helpful to an opera company, but should never be essential to it.

Out of the arrogance and power and egotism and imagination of the modern director, a new opera has been born; whether or not we like it is a matter of personal taste, but the director's triumph is a *fait accompli*. The public has accepted this rejuvenated opera and responded to the director's summons.

Now, after fifteen years, Visconti and Wagner are of the passing generation and younger men are stepping in to take their place. Yet all of these younger directors look to the Wagners, to Visconti, and to Walter Felsenstein of the East Berlin Komische Oper for inspiration and even direct guidance. The old guard (as Visconti was with Zeffirelli, as the Wagners are with the students of their Master Classes) can be immensely helpful in launching careers. For despite the current fad for directors, the opera road is often discouraging for the beginning *régisseur*. Even the big opera organizations sometimes put up a long, tenacious resistance to directors, knowing that they ask high fees and often take over the entire company during the production period. Naturally the smaller opera group, which can never hope to engage Wagner or Visconti or Felsenstein, is even more reluctant to pay an unknown director.

Typical of the younger ranks are men like Jacques Chwat, European-born, now an American citizen, graduate of Columbia College and Yale School of Drama, member of the Bayreuth Master Classes, and disciple of Felsenstein; or Ian Strasfogel, American-born, raised in the theater (his father is a conductor at the Metropolitan), graduate of American universities, but a disciple of the European masters.

These young men are bursting with ideas—operas must not be staged just for the arias; the arias must come from within; the public must be trained to accept modern *régie;* opera ought to be done in the vernacular, because language is the most important element of the art; every moment onstage must ring true; we must follow the path of Verdi and Wagner in making each performance an *oeuvre complète* rather than a vehicle for individual display. Young directors have a contribution to make to the opera stage, a contribution perhaps more valuable in the end than the brilliant flashes of more famous directors. But Chwat, Strasfogel, and their colleagues find the field overcrowded and work scarce. They are not famous enough to be constantly sought, and they sometimes lack the purely technical know-how which would make them stage mechanics or "stage directors." Like young conductors, they work against handicaps which singers never face.

"I spend four months of the year working, and eight months looking for work," says Chwat. "What I make supports me, but barely, barely." Instead of being able to focus upon opera, these young directors must accept television jobs as assistant or associate directors on inane programs which they too often loathe. At best, they resort to off-Broadway productions or university theaters (teaching on the side), but these are considered dead ends. The situation ultimately weakens opera at a time when opera urgently needs fresh talent.

Whether the era of the director has just begun or whether it is on the wane, no one can say. Everyone agrees to a greater or lesser degree that the director is important, most especially when he breathes new life into the "ham and eggs" repertoire which draws the biggest public. Yet many operas now are ridiculously overdirected.

"The exaggerated importance given to the *régie* reduces the drama and the characters to the level of a puppet show," writes *Le Monde* angrily, protesting a Zeffirelli production.

"Directors will go to any lengths to sacrifice every composer, every musician, every score to their will," declares an outraged European operatic administrator who prefers to remain anonymous, fearing the vendetta of the clique of famous *régisseurs*.

Too often the action and décor swamp the music. Too often the composer's explicit wishes are violated. Too often the specifics of the libretto are ignored, leaving the singer embarrassedly mouthing a phrase such as "Terrified, I am transfixed by his awful stare" (*Otello*, Act III, Desdemona to herself during the interview with Otello) while the director orders her to stare at the floor and wring her hands. Too often the very score is torn apart: Verdi would never recognize the Metropolitan edition of *La Forza del Destino*.

Perhaps a moment of balance will eventually be reached, although the critics' war against directors may push *régie* out of the theatrical scene before that moment comes. What is obviously needed is a neater collaboration between pit and stage, voice and action, libretto and score. The public must be retrained to listen to the music, not to look at the stage. Administrators must sacrifice some of their love for splendid productions, remembering that Verdi's career—the most successful in the history of opera—was launched with *Nabucco*, staged with second-hand settings, and costumes left over from a biblical ballet of the previous season. Opera has reached *il ridicolo* when the décor costs more than the music.

Verdi foresaw this when in 1892 he wrote this indictment of "spectacular *mise en scène*": "I detest it. We need just what is necessary, and nothing more. With these big *mises-en-scène*, they will end up doing the same thing over and over again. Big box-offices . . . masses of people . . . and *addio!* drama and music!! They then become secondary items."

We have now reached this point; and in a certain sense we may be said to be in another baroque age, for the overpowering setting and direction make one think of the Bibienas and their contemporaries, who designed to impress the public, not to content the composer. The current vogue of "camp" and its concomitant love for décor over content, let no one forget, has brought reinforcements to the aid of the director and designer. The designs of a Rolf Gérard or a Eugene Berman are not intended to overwhelm the music; the settings of a Beni Montrésor often cannot help doing so. This does not detract one iota from the magic of Montrésor's art, which is undeniably of the highest quality, a sheer enchantment. But such an art is not needed in opera, where the fabric of music and play ought to carry the evening. Opera was intended from the start to be drama with music, not décor and direction with subsidiary drama and music. Not until we are able to see these problems clearly and reach a long-overdue balance in this area will opera come close again to the high ideals set for it by Renaissance humanists: They—deceived idealists—hoped that it might some day become the perfect art.

CHAPTER

IX

THE COMPOSER AND
HOW HE WORKS

Within the closed circle of the music business, the composer alone is a creator. Everyone else merely rephrases or reinterprets what he writes. He alone is the true artist. The others are performers. *"Recitar!"* cries Canio in the *Pagliacci* recitative. "Perform!" This is the traditional lot of both singer and conductor, who may be craftsmen but can never be creators. Only the composer begins with nothing, a void, and shapes a work of art from it.

The composer's position has only lately been acquired, historically speaking; for from Greek and Roman times until the Renaissance he was a figure of minor importance in the theater, usually anonymous, often classed with servants (or slaves) on the social scale. His music, unfortunately, was the merest handmaid of drama.

Only in the late Renaissance did the composer begin to emerge, to struggle toward a position of some dignity; nevertheless, he still remained an accessory in the theatrical scheme. Even so considerable a genius as Claudio Monteverdi ranked below the singer in importance, and the stage marvels of the theatrical engineer meant more to the public than that music which we now consider sublime.

True, the composer then was a paid artist, but more frequently he was recognized as a singer or instrumentalist rather

than as a writer of scores. He still lived in that nether world
reserved for performers. As late as the eighteenth century,
when sculptors and painters were being buried in tombs more
grandiose than those of their own monarchs, theater people
could not yet be buried in hallowed ground. Mozart was given
a pauper's funeral. Only a handful of people followed the
hearse to his wretched grave, whose site is now unknown. But
when Verdi died, a hundred thousand people turned out for
his funeral. All work stopped in Milan that day, and a chorus of
eight hundred voices under Toscanini's baton sang Verdi to his
tomb in the Casa di Riposo, which the composer himself had
built with the millions he had earned in opera. Thus drastically had the music world changed in just one century.

The composer's prestige grew significantly in the seventeenth
century after the opening of the first public opera houses. No
longer merely an employee or servant of a prince-Maecenas,
he suddenly broke free as an independent operator, a professional who could choose his own engagements and accept or
reject commissions at will. The craze for opera gave him all the
work he could use and made him a kind of specialist.

The impresario was the chief influence in the composer's life
during these early years of opera, exercising a tyranny which a
modern composer would not tolerate. Both libretto and librettist were imposed on the composer from above, from the theater
management. The composer could not even choose his own
singers. Instead, he had to work with whatever company was
already under contract. Verdi's correspondence with the management of La Fenice in Venice as late as 1852-53 proves how
long and how hard composers had to fight to win even the
small liberty of selecting the performers they wanted. Yet after
the composer had conquered the impresario, there still remained the battles to be fought with the singers themselves.

Despite all this, the composer's rise was rapid enough. The
year 1647 found Luigi Rossi still employed as the family
musician of the Barberinis in Rome; but by 1658, scarcely a
decade later Pietro Francesco Cavalli had become a free-work-
ing professional. Strong as he was, however, he still continued
his ties as organist and teacher with churches and conserva-

tories, as if he could not believe the luck which had befallen him. Cavalli retained his permanent position with St. Mark's in Venice until the end of his life, although he could have lived on the fees from the thirty-eight operas which he composed. Like Monteverdi before him, Cavalli wrote for both church and stage. And as late as 1720, Vivaldi was to be counted among these *maestri di cappella,* having accepted the invitation of Prince Philip of Hesse-Darmstadt to join the court circle in Mantua. He could, however, accept whatever contracts he liked outside the city, and was allowed to tour from one theater to another, supervising the premières of his operas. Not until 1740 did Vivaldi finally break completely with the convent-orphan-age of Santa Maria della Pietà in Venice, where he had taught and composed for thirty-seven years.

Mozart's long tours and ventures as an independent artist sustained him for a while, yet he was ultimately forced back into service, first with the Archbishop of Salzburg and later with the Emperor in Vienna. Thus Mozart in the eighteenth century was scarcely better off than Monteverdi nearly two hundred years before. His letters to Puchberg document his misery and frustration.

Between the death of Mozart in 1791 and the death of Puccini in 1924, the Golden Age of opera unrolled, decade after luminous decade, première after glittering première, until the composer became a veritable god. During this era, composers almost stumbled over one another in their frenzy to be heard by opera-mad audiences. Then the composer reached his full stature. He was master of the theater, *Il Maestro,* writing as impulse and inspiration dictated, writing for whom he pleased.

Aided by the music publisher, whose influence swelled throughout the 1800's, the composer could negotiate from a position of absolute power. Toward the middle of the nine-teenth century, he could select his own subject and librettist, or he could write his own librettos, as Wagner did. This was a great victory; even as late as 1829, the celebrated composer Bellini had a libretto forced on him by a theater management: *Zaira,* written for the inauguration of the Regio in Parma.

Finally the composer was freed of the old slavery. His score could take precedence over vocal pyrotechnics. Under the direction of the composer himself, a drama could emerge based on the combined effort of a whole company. And if a composer wrote for a certain singer, it was because that singer could *serve* his music, be molded to fit the drama as the composer conceived it.

The rise of the conductor, too, enabled the composer to divorce himself still further from any tie with a given theater; for the conductor, almost invariably a man of superior intelligence, could take over the task of putting the opera together and getting it onstage, freeing the composer for new work.

No longer did the composer need a rich patron in order to survive. Backed by his music publisher, he could protect his author's rights, fight against the piracy and plagiarism common to the time, and dictate an absolute law on where and when and by whom his works might be performed. Vivaldi and Cavalli must often have wished for such a situation, but they were powerless to protect themselves. Had they only lived in the tumultuous period of Verdi's edicts against La Scala, which—incredibly—was reduced to begging the composer for his scores and being refused!

Backed by a firm such as Ricordi or Schirmer, Lucca or Sonzogno, Schott, or Breitkopf and Härtel, the composer could defend his work and earn from it year after year—a thing he had never been able to do before. Previously the composer had been paid once (by the commissioning impresario or theater) for an opera, no matter how successful it was or how often performed. His income had depended on his output—upon the number of operas he composed, rather than on the number of times each work was performed. After the composer and publisher began working together, the same work could earn over and over again for its creator.

The music publishing house, which had sole power to lease out a given composer's scores, could also force a certain theater to buy the rights to perform lesser, newer, or older works before it would release the current popular opera for performance. For example, a theater which wanted to put on *Rigo-*

letto might be forced by Verdi's publisher to stage another, less popular Verdi work in the same season (and pay well for the right to produce it). Or to take another example, Mascagni's publisher might force a theater to produce the opera of some new, unknown composer in order to get the rights to perform *Cavalleria*. It is almost impossible to overstate the importance of the music publishing house in shaping the fate of operas and their composers. A comparison of five careers shows how composers' destinies were altered in the course of three centuries:

Pietro Francesco Cavalli: 39 operas between 1639 and 1654
Niccolò Jommelli: 55 operas between 1737 and 1774
Gaetano Donizetti: 75 operas between 1839 and 1893
Giuseppe Verdi: 27 operas between 1839 and 1893
Giacomo Puccini: 10 operas between 1884 and 1926 (date of completed *Turandot*)

Here are three centuries in profile. The prodigious activity of the early composers is reflected against the slow working pace which Puccini could permit himself. The turning point came in Verdi's lifetime. In one year alone (1645) Cavalli wrote and produced three operas. A whole century later (in 1746) Niccolò Jommelli still was working at this speed. Donizetti passed them both, composing four works in 1822, four in 1826, four in 1828, four in 1830, and four in 1832. But Verdi, scarcely twenty years later, could allow himself two entire years for *I Vespri Siciliani*, two for *Simone Boccanegra*, three for *Forza*, five for *Don Carlo*, four for *Aida*. All the while, he was earning regularly and steadily from his works, and was in the envious position of being able to turn down offers from theaters and conservatories which wanted him to become their director.

After Verdi's day, the composer could write relatively little and still become rich, provided his operas were popular. Puccini's output totals less than one-fifth of Jommelli's, one-seventh of Donizetti's. But Puccini, like Verdi, was able to live from what he earned in opera.

In spite of this gradual diminishing of the composer's activity, the market for opera remained strong, the mania reaching its apex in the premières of Verdi's *Otello* and *Falstaff,* of Puccini's *Fanciulla* at the Metropolitan, and finally of the post-humous *Turandot* at La Scala. Toscanini conducted this work for an international public on the night of April 25, 1925. At that point in the score where death ended Puccini's career, Toscanini laid down his baton and addressed the Milanese public: "This is the end of the opera, unfinished because here Maestro died."

At that moment, a funeral oration for the art of operatic composition would have been in order, for the promise of Mascagni and Francesco Cilèa and Umberto Giordano had already been fulfilled to a considerable extent, and there appeared to be no one left to carry on the tradition. Opera, as the public had known it up to that time, seemed to be dead.

A long lapse in the continuity of operatic composing followed. Today, thirty years after that historic night in Milan, the full-time opera composer has almost completely disappeared from the theatrical scene, paradoxically at a time when opera appears to be flourishing and a new vogue for opera appears to have been launched.

The paradox is double, and complex; for the old order of music has been upset. In the eighteenth century it was easier to earn a living writing operas than composing for instruments alone. Today the reverse is true. It is very nearly impossible to stay alive on opera royalties. The *Enciclopedia dello Spettacolo* lists only Gian-Carlo Menotti as the sole survivor of a once-hardy race. Menotti himself would include Britten and perhaps Orff in the list of full-time opera composers; but in fact both men are subsidized in one way or another, and Menotti is the only opera composer to live on royalties alone, as composers formerly did.

The paradox has yet another aspect: financially composers of all kinds are better off than ever before in history. It is difficult to find an indigent composer, one who is as poor as Mozart and Vivaldi were. No composer of the early nineteenth century was really rich; not even Bellini or Donizetti, famous as they were, could be called rich, or even comfortably secure, because both men died before they could reap the benefits of authors'-

rights laws. But from Verdi to Puccini to Strauss, Stravinsky, Menotti, Barber, and Britten, composers have been well off, occupying a niche in social and intellectual circles more comfortable than that of their predecessors. They travel in style, live well, lodge away from home in de luxe hotels or villas or *palazzi*, have city apartments and country houses. They employ servants at a time when many singers, even some of considerable reputation, are reduced to doing their own housework with the aid of part-time cleaning women. Composers buy paintings, collect antiques and fine books, dress well. (Almost the only exception to this rule is the Venetian Luigi Nono, whose trademarks are unpressed pants, colored sweat shirts, and a house in a poor quarter of the city.) On the whole, the composer of today enjoys having his dignity and position respected as never before. And still it is impossible to make a living composing operas. This is a problem certain foundations might be well advised to study before they invest further in buildings to house new operas. If Menotti is, as the *Enciclopedia* says, the sole working composer of operas, something has gone awry since 1920. Composers ought to be able to live from their chosen profession, as a physician does. No one expects a doctor to moonlight as a truck driver or insurance salesman. The composer ought to enjoy similar security.

Italians call Menotti an "American musician," while Americans tend to think of him as Italian. As his operas prove, he has absorbed both cultures. Born near Como, on July 7, 1911, he is now in his mid-fifties. Verdi at this age had reached the landmark of *Don Carlo;* Rossini's entire career as composer was ended; Wagner at fifty-three had written *Lohengrin, Tannhäuser, Der Fliegende Holländer, Tristan,* and *Meistersinger*. Menotti's own career to date is marked by the following operatic works:

> *Amelia Goes to the Ball* (1937)
> *The Old Maid and the Thief* (1939)
> *The Island God* (1942)
> *The Medium* (1946)
> *The Telephone* (1947)
> *The Consul* (1950)

Amahl and the Night Visitors (1951)
The Saint of Bleecker Street (1954)
Maria Golovin (1958)
libretto of *Vanessa* [music by Samuel Barber] (1958)
Labyrinth (1963)
The Last Savage (1963)
Martin's Lie (1964)

It is a distinguished record, especially since three of these are the most frequently performed operas of this generation; another, *The Consul,* won both the New York Critics' Circle Award and the Pulitzer Prize for music. Translated into twenty-three languages, it is still being performed all over the world and has won a place in the permanent repertory. *Amahl, The Medium,* and *The Telephone* are only slightly less popular. No other contemporary opera composer can match this record; only Britten approaches it. Pizzetti's output is large enough, but his works are not frequently performed, even in Italy. Egk, Hans Werner Henze, Dallapiccola, and Orff have together composed only a handful of works, and of these only one or two are currently played, while not even one has entered the popular repertory.

Menotti's success can first be explained in terms of his genius as a man of the theater. Librettist, composer, director of his own works and those of other composers, he is a kind of Renaissance man. The hallmarks of his art are his transparent, almost childlike simplicity—which is irresistible—his humanity, and his immediate accessibility. Anyone can understand Menotti, a fact which irritates some of his colleagues, whose baffling music seems to have been written solely for self-gratification. Living in the era of abstract art, Menotti should be following the vogues of the day, if he is to be in style; but he does not. For twenty-five years, he has remained obstinately apart from all the current fads in musical composition, working steadily toward private goals. In this age of noncommunication, Menotti wishes only to communicate, to reach out across the orchestra and seize his public.

Toscanini called *The Medium* a masterpiece. *Amahl* moved him to tears. *The Last Savage* makes the audience laugh out loud. Menotti's public reacts to a composer who is unabashedly sentimental. While other composers are playing it cool, Menotti burns hot, like Italians of the great tradition. He is not ashamed to laugh and cry. But the adherents of more abstract music refuse to consider him seriously.

"My commitment to the human heart seems to irritate some of my colleagues," Menotti says mildly. "Emotion is out of fashion, it seems."

Twelve-toners resent his popularity. Academicians mistrust him because he is free and untrammeled: Menotti rarely follows the same path twice. Obscurantists fear him because he is relatively clear. Computer musicians dislike his warmth. Self-appointed "serious" composers of the closed circle mock him because he makes a wholehearted effort to reach his public.

Menotti's enemies are many and voluble. The following examples from the body of criticism of Menotti's art are by no means the most vitriolic, but they give a fair sample of what Menotti regularly expects when he opens the newspapers:

Igor Stravinsky, writing in *Show* Magazine:

"A not very good composer at his not infrequent worst . . . A piece of corn [*The Last Savage*] . . . The latter two thirds of this score should have been composed by feeding the first third into an IBM machine."

Guido Pannain, reviewing *The Consul* for an Italian daily:

"A detective drama, swollen with presumption . . . Old stuff, positively antique . . . There is no real and true music in it. Think of a bad movie adapted to the opera stage with musical accompaniment hauled out of a half-century of rotten music . . . His music is an anthology of bad taste."

Pannain, reviewing *Amahl*:

"With *Amahl*, he brings us comic strip opera. The music of Menotti is a kind of provincial samples fair, so light and so forgettable that it is not even worth being taken seriously . . . But unfortunately Menotti is a part of the life and the musical culture of our times, and so this becomes a serious thing which has to be taken seriously . . ."

Edmund Tracey, reviewing *Martin's Lie* for an English daily:

". . . watered-down Puccini . . . My final impression was one of resentment."

And, finally, Clarendon in *Le Figaro*, reviewing the world première of *The Last Savage:*

". . . painful, extremely poor—so poor as to border on bankruptcy . . . An operetta *manquée* . . . Menotti had the right to make it simple, but he did not have the right to make it poor . . . The public will have a hard time believing that tax money was used to put on such a miserable work . . ."

When Menotti read the last of these, in Paris, he said: "If I were a young composer just starting out, I would never write music again."

Shortly afterward, Janet Flanner restored something like proper perspective to the scene with her own analysis of *The Last Savage,* which appeared in the November 2, 1963 issue of *The New Yorker:*

"Letter from Paris"—October 23, 1963

Le Dernier Sauvage, an *opera bouffe* by Gian-Carlo Menotti was given its official première this week at the Opéra Comique. It was commissioned for the house by the Comique, now directed by the composer, Georges Auric, as part of a renovation plan to bring modern blood and fresh musical sounds to the dust of its repertory and stage. The libretto, also written by Menotti, in a satiric vein, is elaborate and very funny, especially to Americans, the best equipped to appreciate the gaiety of its parody of themselves.

On the whole, the première audience seemed to enjoy itself immensely—all except the critics. Being an *opera bouffe, The Last Savage* will not have the popularity of *The Consul* with the visible and audible tragedy of the postwar displaced people whose very lives hung on a visa. Nor will it vie with *The Medium,* with its hypnotic music and its charlatanism in respect to the hereafter. Both of these earlier works are basic, specific, uncostumed modern tragedies. . . . They are operas of small individuals' sufferings, and the Menotti music deeply orchestrates their modest human feelings. It would seem that his special exceptional gift is to write brief, vivid Grand Guignol-esque plays with the *brio* of the great theater man he is, and to set them to his emotional, melodic music.

Act I of *The Last Savage* could probably be shortened to advantage. In his parody spirit, Menotti has also included parody snatches of the opera masters. Thus, he brought in new hindsights on Rossini, made occasional open use of Puccini, produced sextets and septets, and often oddly interrupted the flow of his own creation with rich trumpet calls and musical flourishes, as if something new were coming, perhaps an aria, though none emerges until the last act, which contains beautiful musical writing. The Paris music critics have already used Menotti rather as their whipping boy. In their reports on this week's Menotti opera, it is they who have been the savages.

—Genêt

In spite of all that has been written about them, the public pays to go to Menotti's operas. Pays, laughs, cries, applauds. In the theater, little else counts. "When the public does not run to a new production, it is already a failure . . ." This, from a Verdi letter of 1899. It was a creed Verdi held throughout his career; and the continuing life of his operas proves him right. Nothing counts save public response.

Because Menotti belongs so completely to opera, and opera in the modern sense to him, because he lives and breathes the theater as no part-time composer, part-time teacher can, his whole existence is a document of the way an opera composer works. A study of his daily routine gives insight into what the composer's life once was, what it might be again if opera composing again becomes a viable trade.

Here is a cross-section of Menotti's days, traced during the creation and production of *The Last Savage*. The work was commissioned in 1959 for the Paris Opéra by Georges Hirsch, former administrator of the French National Theaters. Originally titled *The Last Superman*, it was intended to be *"Les Indes Galantes* of our own epoch," according to Hirsch. Menotti accepted the commission with the idea of writing a comic opera in the tradition of Donizetti.

Work on the *Savage* was scarcely under way when the French theater administration changed, presaging trouble. Menotti was advised by the new management that a comic work could not be staged at the Opéra. The *Savage* was handed over to Herve Dugardin of the Opéra-Comique, and Menotti was forced to reduce the planned *mise en scène*. Next, the French translation done by Menotti's own translator proved inadequate to the Comique, so large sections of the work had to be retranslated. The composer himself, overwhelmed with other work on *Labyrinth* for CBS and *The Death of the Bishop of Brindisi* for the Cincinnati May Festival, in addition to his duties as director and founder of the Festival of Two Worlds in Spoleto, was delayed in completing the orchestration. But after many postponements and changes of plans, *The Last Savage* was finally scheduled for the 1963 autumn season of the Comique. The Metropolitan had already put it on the program for 1964-65 and planned to offer its American première in January. La Fenice of Venice agreed to do the Italian première of the work, which was then to go on to Palermo and other theaters of the Italian Ente Nazionale. Thus Menotti had three premières of the *Savage* and the world première of *Martin's Lie* on his calendar for a seven-month period in the fall-winter-spring of 1963-64, all to be directed and rehearsed by him. In his "spare" time, he expected to put together the 1964 Spoleto Festival, which was to open ten days after the *Martin* première in England.

Menotti left for Paris right after the 1963 Spoleto Festival, registered at his hotel, and went directly to the Comique to begin rehearsing his French cast. Nearly two months of work were required, for scenery, costumes, and score were all new to the singers who were, in turn, new to Menotti. The fact that all save two were French, and that they were all professionals, eased his job considerably. Even so, there were many changes to be made to suit the opera to the stage, the cast, and the management, and to shape the stage and cast and orchestra to Menotti's wishes.

As the première drew near, Menotti's days grew longer. Associates, friends, critics, singers, directors, came from America and Europe for the first Menotti stage première since *Maria Golovin* had been offered in 1958 at the Brussels World's Fair. The composer's usual six or seven hours of sleep were reduced to five hours, sometimes four. Added tensions resulted from the fact that Paris planned not one première, but two. The first, a gala charity benefit which counted the Duke and Duchess of Windsor and several hundred international jet-set and diplomatic-circle celebrities in its audience, was to be followed one night later by the "true" première, the first public performance of the much-discussed *Le Dernier Sauvage*.

Both premières were successful with the public. Menotti had again won *le tout-Paris* which had first claimed him as its darling in the postwar years, after the Occupation, when an American troupe played *The Medium* and *The Telephone* at the Théâtre de la Renaissance. On the first night of that production, there were only twenty-odd people in the theater, but those twenty proclaimed a "new renaissance for the old art of opera" in Menotti's work, and he became the vogue in Paris almost overnight. His name was paired with that of Jean-Paul Sartre and Albert Camus: he was the voice of the *après-guerre*. Now he had brought *Le Sauvage* to Paris and had scored another triumph—he thought.

The next morning brought shock and disillusionment. Most of the critics were very hostile to the work. True, *Paris Match* and the widely read *Le Monde* were favorable to the opera. *Match* called Menotti the greatest opera composer of our time; while René Dumesnil, the dean of French critics, writing in *Le Monde,* spoke very graciously of both *Savage* and composer. Still, most of the other reviews were bad. Menotti, in the days remaining to him in Paris, was sad and discouraged. Even after twenty-five years in the theater, he is not yet resigned to critics' shafts. He left Paris with the applause of the public ringing in his head and the taste of the reviews sour in his mouth.

Back in New York at the beginning of November (after a stop in London to straighten out some matters relating to the *Martin's Lie* première), Menotti was plunged first into Spoleto Festival planning sessions. But the American première of the *Savage* was scarcely more than two months away, and there

were changes to be made in the score even before the early
room rehearsals could start. More work, then again the round
of coaching sessions, group rehearsals, action plotting, rehearsals with piano, rehearsals with orchestra, and finally the
first pasting together of all the parts. This time the work was
done in English, not French, so for all practical purposes
Menotti was dealing with another libretto. The scenery and
costumes, too, were new, having been designed and executed
in New York especially for the Metropolitan production of the
Savage.

At the Met, as in Paris, Menotti had a cast of experts who
loved the work and had an old-fashioned good time. The Met
became "the merriest place in town," according to a *New
Yorker* reporter.

"FUN FOR ALL," runs the *New Yorker* headline. Word gets
around New York that a success is in the making. The public
begins a run on tickets.

The actual première is a success. Menotti smiles again. "A
simply delightful evening," writes Alan Rich in the New York
Herald-Tribune; "there comes a time when high aesthetic prin-
ciples must be thrown to the winds, and this, dear reader, is
the time . . . The audience loved it all the way. When Menotti
appeared at the final curtain, the crowd erupted as though he
were Maria Callas." *The New York Times* critic is not so kind:
he sounds more like the reviewers Menotti is accustomed to
reading. But the most important thing—and let no one forget
it—is that the public enjoyed itself.

"My only merit is that I hold out my hand to a public which
is discouraged by hermetic modern music," Menotti says.

Within a week, tickets for *The Last Savage* are hard to find
on the New York market. The success of the opera is made in
America. But by now it is February, and Menotti is due in
Venice, where the Italian première has to be prepared.

He arrives in Italy in time for conferences on the 1964 Festival of Two Worlds, then goes on to Venice, to the Teatro La
Fenice, arriving at eleven in the morning, when the theater is
just beginning to come to life. But Menotti has gotten up at
six to take the seven A.M. *rapido* from Milan.

Within a few moments he learns that there is trouble. The artist chosen to design the sets will probably not be able to work on the Italian production. Menotti tries to set things to rights with an international telephone call, but the problems cannot be worked out. He has to leave Venice to return to New York. The theater assures him that they will get a scenic designer and have everything ready for his return.

April 17, 1964: Menotti back in Venice. He arrives expecting to find everything in order—or, at the very worst, to find preliminary sketches and designs ready and to find the cast waiting for him. But the only thing La Fenice has to offer are two bad photostats of sketches by a well-known Italian stage designer who has misunderstood the meaning of the *Savage* and dashed off a *Lakmé*-like drawing which Menotti rejects at once. The search is on again for a scenery-and-costume director. Menotti also finds the baritone unsatisfactory, so auditions begin for a Savage. The baritone, being the protagonist, must be able to carry much of the opera alone. Back in his hotel, Menotti must consider the problems arising from the *Martin's Lie* première, where he is also lacking a protagonist. But even at the end of this tiring first day in Venice, it is back to the theater in the evening for the first rehearsal. The management takes him on a tour of the theater to show him various sketches by Italian scene designers. He chooses the artist who seems most likely to understand the *Savage*. He also considers candidates for the role of Savage. After some thought, Menotti decides to telephone New York for John Reardon of the New York City Opera. Reardon accepts the job, but he cannot get to Venice before April 30 . . . previous commitments.

April 18: There are orchestra rehearsals and conferences with the business manager of the Spoleto Festival. The *Savage* soprano is not yet there, and she cannot arrive before May 1. Until then, the company will rehearse with a stand-in, American soprano Elena Manè, an expatriate living in Milan. "I always feel better when there are Americans in the cast," says Menotti. The other singers are all young, like Manè, but most of them are working professionals rather than beginners. Not of the class of Mady Mesplé, Gabriel Bacquier, and Solange

Michel (the Paris cast) or of George London, Nicolai Gedda and Roberta Peters (the New York cast), but first-class, intelligent young pros. Menotti is encouraged by this. They take direction well.

April 19: Sunday. Conferences, visitors, telephone calls. Chorus rehearsal.

April 20: Rehearsals with principals, but without chorus. Menotti is working with an American assistant director, teaching him the opera. The secenic designer has come up with some preliminary sketches, but they are earthbound, heavy, wrong. A second rendering is done. Better. But nothing has yet happened on the costumes. The scenic designer decides he cannot do both sets and costumes, so a costumer is called in from Rome.

April 21: Chorus action blocked out. First act onstage with principals. Second chorus rehearsal. Menotti finds chorus lacking in discipline, a fault common to Italian theaters. He goes over the second act with both principals and chorus. It begins to look as if they know what it is all about. One electronic tape is run for the cocktail party scene, but Menotti doesn't like it. A second tape is made, but that too is rejected. Five P.M.: principals and chorus. Eight-thirty: Act III chorus, without principals.

April 23: Goes over Act II three times with the whole cast, and it is really set. But Menotti does not like the baritone who is standing in for Reardon. Wishes Reardon were there. Soprano Manè is good. An excellent mezzo, Greek Rena Garazioti, a top-flight young professional in the Italian theater circuit, is the Maharanee.

April 24: To Torcello for lunch. The first break Menotti has taken since his arrival in Venice, but this too is a business appointment. Afternoon and evening rehearsals with principals and chorus. Menotti hands over part of one rehearsal to an assistant, but when he leaves the theater discipline breaks down. Principals protest when asked to go over scenes.

April 25: No rehearsal, but whole day spent in conferences about scenery and costumes. Menotti, for no reason, is suddenly preoccupied with the idea of his own death. "I don't have enough time. What if I should die tomorrow? I haven't accomplished anything, but I have passed the age where I can look forward to life." (Verdi said the same thing nearly a decade before he wrote *Otello* and *Falstaff*.)

April 26: Back to rehearsals. The chorus botches the cocktail party scene because they have never been to a cocktail party and have no idea what one is like. They don't know how to hold cocktail glasses and drink from them. They throw down the drinks in one shot, as if they were *ombrettas* of Venetian red. "You act like a *Traviata* chorus," Menotti shouts at them. "Or worse: *Cavalleria*." Working with the principals, he tries to get proper shades of humor without farce. There are repeats and repeats to get the correct phrasing and inflection. The bass goes over a tricky phrase ten, fifteen, twenty times. Menotti teaches the soprano how to breathe. But the other principals get restless, and the noise level mounts. The women's spike heels pound on the wood floors of the rehearsal hall. "Please, please don't talk," Menotti shouts. "Silence," echo some of the principals, as the rehearsal pianist begins to play again. The tenor muffs his interpretation: he is thinking only of the high note (an A, actually, and not very high) which lies ahead in the score. Menotti stamps his foot and runs thin nervous fingers through his hair. The big ensemble begins to fall apart: all six principals are tired. Menotti has two assistants now, one of his own, imported from New York, and one assigned by the theater. Still he insists on doing everything himself. In the scene with Kitty, the Prince, Sardula, Scattergood, Maharajah, and Maharanee in Act I, there is a complex pattern of movement which matches the music. The stage is divided by a wall. "You make two slow turns around the stage, then front, then around again, then front, then around again," Menotti directs the soprano. Manè protests, "You have to be an Einstein to follow this." She is not far from wrong. Menotti has his own ideas about direction. He writes words and music together (instead of taking a prewritten libretto and fitting music to it), and as he works on the composition he has the action already plotted out in his mind. He knows exactly how he wants it done, how he can get maximum effects by combining musical climaxes with action climaxes. After long, tiring hours of rehearsal, Menotti goes to listen to a third trial of the tape for the electronics-music parody. Then to the designer's apartment to see how the set designs are coming. Menotti is beginning to be happy about them.

April 27: Rehearsals all day. Opening scene of Act II. Much confusion. Menotti goes over the early parts of the scene five times without much success. He doesn't even get the duet of soprano and baritone. Everyone is still waiting for Reardon. But Menotti is patient: "We must give them the skeleton first, then add the flesh."

April 28: Menotti works on *Martin's Lie* orchestration. Because England is pressing him for it, it cannot be postponed any longer. *Savage* rehearsals in afternoon. Act III with music only, no movement. Menotti is still making changes in the score, which has been much cut since the Paris première. The duet from Act I, Scene 2, has been taken out, which Menotti regrets. "I would like to use it somewhere else." He thinks about where it might be worked in, for it seems too good to toss away.

April 29: Menotti rejects the soprano originally chosen for the bit part of the Lieder Singer in the cocktail party scene. "Her voice is too pretty, not hard and strong enough. I really want a heavier voice." By now rehearsals are taking eight to ten hours of Menotti's day.

April 30: Still on the cocktail party. The chorus master has chosen middle-aged women to play the parts of the debs. Menotti cannot accept this. He must switch all chorus solo roles around, but do it gracefully so that no one will be offended. Also, he must not hurt the chorus master's feelings. Reardon arrives.

May 1: Where is the scenery? When will it be ready? Only a few random pieces have been brought in. Friday is traditionally an unlucky day. The soprano arrives and does not know any of the score. Opening night is only two weeks away. She admits she probably cannot learn the score in time, so the role is given to Manè, who is there and ready to sing. Good break for Manè. Reardon, on the other hand, arrives with all the music and words committed to memory. Garazioti and Paolo Washington are also prepared. All the singers are enthusiastic about the music. It is singable: in the Italian, *orecchiabile*, "It fits the ear." Bits and pieces of the score are beginning to be heard in cafés around the theater: people are picking it up, whistling and humming it, as they did Verdi's music when he rehearsed there.

May 2: Rehearsal with principals and orchestra. Followed by rehearsal with *comprimarios*. Followed by rehearsal with chorus and principals. Followed by rehearsal of whole company with orchestra. Conductor is Carlo Franci, strong on new operas. Menotti is worried: one day he says things are going well, the next day everything is a disaster. "I don't know whether I am more afraid of empty houses or of a bad performance," he admits. Venetian audiences are often cold. What if they don't applaud at all? Menotti is frightened of Italy. He was badly burned at La Scala when *The Consul* was premièred there and was greeted by a gang of anti-Menottists equipped with children's police whistles, determined to whistle the opera off the stage. Rumor comes to Venice that the same clique is prepared to wreck the *Savage*.

May 3: Further worries about costumes and scenery. No one has seen tangible evidence that anything is being done. Lots of promises from the management—tomorrow and always tomorrow—but nothing yet. It is Sunday. No rehearsals. Menotti works on *Martin's Lie* all day. In the past week he has had to work on it after midnight and from seven to ten in the morning.

May 4: Spring has arrived, and everyone has spring fever. But Menotti, who has been trying for three weeks to find time for an hour-long stroll through Venice, is still bound to his work. There are rehearsals all day: cast with piano and conductor; stress on accent, tone, inflection, interpretation. These are the fine lines being drawn in now that everyone has the music and the action in his head. In questions of diction, Menotti is a perfectionist. To a singer who has to sing *"bene,"* and who for vocal reasons broadens his vowels, he is inflexible: "No, no! The word is *'be-ne'* not *'bah-nah,'*" Menotti yells. "*'Bay-nay,'* no that's not right. Can't you pronounce your own language? *'Bay-*

nay.' Again. No, again. Once more. Don't swallow the sound."
Then he turns to another singer, who must pronounce the word
tristezza—"sadness." Fifteen minutes are spent getting her to
sound "sad but not tragic." "Not so heavy," Menotti cries. "Remember this is a comedy: not *Trovatore.*" "Too heavy. Too
intense." He lightens the overly heavy action (the singers are
accustomed to singing in tragedies) so that it suits the music.
"Don't waddle. Walk!" "Why do you run now? Not so fast.
Slow it down."

May 5: The *Savage* has been dividing the stage with *Norma*
rehearsals; but now the Menotti singers would like to have the
stage all the time. It is not possible. The regular *stagione* is
under way and onstage time is strictly rationed. Room rehearsal
today. Menotti is cranky with singers. When one of the principals slurs through a line (on the tenth or twelfth repetition of
a scene), Menotti becomes angry with her. "Either you perform
or you don't perform. This is no picnic. No slipshod work will
do." She becomes petulant but capitulates to him. From now
on she sings it perfectly every time. In every minute not used
for rehearsals, Menotti is working on *Martin;* that première is
scheduled for one month from today.

May 6: For the first time in a month, Menotti catches up on
his correspondence. He reads all his mail but rarely finds time
to answer. Between morning rehearsals and afternoon rehearsals, he sandwiches in an hour of letter writing, but he has
to skip lunch to do it. In that hour, he receives four long-
distance phone calls. (The hotel desk shunts off two or three
calls for every one he actually receives.) Afternoon and evening
rehearsals. General panic about costumes and scenery. Only a
third of the scenery is ready, and none of the costumes are
finished. Some of the singers have not even been measured.

May 7: Holiday—Feast of the Ascension—but work goes on
in rehearsals with orchestra, chorus, principals, stage. All day
filled because *Norma* cast has day of rest. Singers are beginning
to tire. Nerves take over.

May 8: The cast is in summer clothes, for spring has come
and gone in a week. To the usual aggravations are added heat
and summer flu. Menotti's agent has arrived from New York

with a briefcaseful of problems relating to future plans. In the rehearsal breaks, Menotti must think about *Martin* and about the Vienna première of *The Death of the Bishop of Brindisi,* scheduled for June 10. Spoleto opens June 15. Still no costumes and sets for *Savage,* and the première is only one week from today.

May 9: The conductor has to fill in for the *Norma* conductor, who is sick. Thus all *Savage* rehearsals are moved around, and Franci is always tired. It is hard to sustain a performance on-stage and a performance in production simultaneously. Menotti is worrying more and more about chances for success. The soprano singing Kitty is frightened; nerves nearly a week in advance. Menotti takes time to reassure her, and talks with mezzo Garazioti about possible future engagement as Magda in Greek production of *Consul.*

May 10: "Have you seen any of your costumes?" "Not a stitch." Nor is the scenery ready. Menotti is frantic. "How can you expect these singers to do a new opera without having seen all the sets onstage?" He argues with the management; the answer, as always, is "Tomorrow." Today is Sunday. No rehearsals. But Franci has a performance of *Norma.* Menotti spends half the day on the telephone, to Rome, to Milan, to Paris, to London, to New York.

May 11: Full day of rehearsals, but no costumes. The wardrobe is working day and night. One set is ready and the props are all delivered. Singers may now begin to rehearse with props for the first time. The music and action are both in good shape, and Menotti is pleased with that, at least. He feels that this may be the best production of the three, better than Paris, where it was sung in French, better than New York, where it was sung in English. Just as he is beginning to be in high spirits, the blow comes: the scenery painters announce that they cannot have the sets ready until the night of the première. Rage. Blow-ups. Arguments, but to no avail. Worse, the conductor is only available for part of the rehearsal. He is tired from *Norma,* which is a major conducting chore. Is the whole thing going to fall apart at the last minute? Characteristically, Menotti's concern is for the young singers involved, not for his own opera.

"Think of the singers," he harangues the La Fenice management. "What a terrible way to introduce them to the world of
opera."

May 12: The *anteprova*, the rehearsal-before-the-dress-re-
hearsal, which is the last private, closed rehearsal, according to
ageless Italian theater custom. By now Menotti has read Stravinsky's attack on him and the *Savage*, for an American ac-
quaintance has left a copy of *Show* Magazine lying where
Menotti could find it. He takes the article philosophically,
though he is saddened—as always—to have to admit that he has
enemies. He likes to be liked. He never gives in to depression,
never takes a defeatist attitude toward either his career or his
work. Tomorrow is the general dress rehearsal. Too late for
tears and recriminations. But the *anteprova* goes very well.
Menotti's singers have learned the score to perfection, and
there are far fewer mistakes than in an ordinary rehearsal of a
standard opera. Perhaps they work harder on these new scores
than they would on *Bohème* or *Traviata*. In any case, frag-
ments of the *Savage* melodies are floating all over Venice, not
just around the theater. The music has already caught on. And
this is why Verdi kept the music to *"La donna è mobile"* a
secret from his *Rigoletto* cast in this same theater, a hundred
and ten years ago. Still no costumes for most of the singers,
though one or two have been brought down from the wardrobe.
The seamstress shouts from the window of the costume room to
her fiancé standing against the wellhead in Campo de la Taverna
below that she is too busy to come out for a drink. Now, when
the parodies of modern music and modern art are paraded on
the stage in the second act, everyone in the theater laughs.
They have caught on, and are now in on the joke. As at the
Met, as at the Comique, everyone in the production is having
a colossally good time. Menotti remarks that the theater is the
perfect size for the production. The spirit of La Fenice is right
too: neither heavy like Paris, nor dark red and big like the Met.
The orchestra, which plays the best *Traviata* in the opera business (and *Traviata* was written for La Fenice), handles the
score with the proper delicacy and sentimentality. It begins to
look as if it will be a perfect production.

May 13: The *prova generale,* which is in truth the first public performance of the work, not a dress rehearsal in the American sense of the word. There is a sizeable audience, including
critics from all over Europe and the usual group of restless,
fashionable première hunters who follow Menotti wherever he
goes. Of course, he is still nervous about bringing a new opera
to Italy. Italian audiences are, as a rule, death on unfamiliar
works, so much so that La Scala admits that it can offer only a
handful each year. But a long, sympathetic article favorable to
Menotti has come out in the Venice paper, filling almost half
a page. This is a good sign. Before the rehearsal begins, Menotti
appears before the curtain to explain that the scenery is not
yet ready. He fills in the gaps by describing the missing sets.
There is a good deal of applause at the end of the first act.
Another good sign. But not everything goes smoothly. The
tenor, whom everyone had counted on to perform without a
flaw, has a bad throat. He cannot get to the top notes and must
leave holes in the score and a bad impression with the audience.
There is no stand-in for his role, so nothing can be done. He
has to get through it as best he can. The rest of the cast is in
top form. The rehearsal is a complete success. But what about
the critics? Menotti will have to wait until May 16 to find out.

May 14: Day of rest for everyone except the composer; but
now *Martin* and *The Bishop* are foremost in his mind. A representative from Vienna is here to negotiate for the Austrian
première of the *Savage.* Palermo and other Italian theaters
want it. New waves of acquaintances come in and have to be
entertained. Menotti takes a half-day to go to the Lido for a
swim at the Bains. First break in nearly a month of work. Some
of the sets are delivered—one day in advance of the première.
The rest will come tomorrow. Singers are seeing their costumes
for the first time, trying their makeup. Manè has first-night
nerves already, but Garazioti and Adriana Maliponte comfort
her. Maliponte was the Paris Sardula, so she has been through
all this before. She is more confident than anyone of its chances
for success. Menotti has reached the stage of don't-care. He
remembers that a celebrated New York theater expert predicted
that *The Consul* would be a disaster—and the opera ran for

eight months at the Ethel Barrymore Theater. He knows from experience that the fate of *Savage* is in the lap of the gods.

May 15: The première. Menotti spends the whole day at the theater, working with the sets and stage crew during the last-minute frenzy of the *prima,* improvising a set for the first act out of bits and pieces of scenery from the second and third acts; setting—a rather surrealistic pavilion which was greeted with enthusiastic applause when the curtain went up. Also, he has to adjust lights at the last minute—with the public outside in the foyer clamoring to be admitted to the auditorium. He barely has time to go back to his hotel to change into evening clothes. Still thinking of everyone else except himself, he hopes that the opera will go "for the singers' sakes." He would hate to see them beaten down in a fiasco. Franci is tired from the *Norma,* but has high hopes for success. He says that Venice, like Trieste and Palermo, tends to receive new music well. If there is a receptive public in Italy for unfamiliar works, it is here. Franci takes the podium: the *Savage* begins on time, and the house is full. Menotti's fear of an empty house was unfounded; now he has only the reaction of the public to worry about. Franci attacks the overture with much gusto. It is Rossininian, and the Venetian public loves it. There is much applause, so the evening is off to a good start. The jokes get laughs. The ensemble and arias get applause, though some of the more sophisticated American humor escapes the Venetian public. But everything goes well: no cues missed, no muffs in the orchestra, smooth acting and singing from all. The evening ends with curtain calls and much applause for everyone, including Menotti, who is satisfied—except for one small item: some of the sets have not yet been delivered. The "tomorrows" have come and gone. Now he is told that the production will be complete for the second performance. After the show he makes the rounds of the dressing rooms, thanking his singers, then goes off exhausted to a small, private party in an old *palazzo.*

May 16: Reviews. Although Menotti denies that he cares, he reads them just the same. He gets up at seven, as always, and reaches for the Venice morning paper. It is a very fair review.

The opera given for the first time in Italian, the original language of Menotti's libretto, has been understood by a wary and critical public and by most of Italy's devastating critics. The consensus is that it is highly singable and rich in music—things all too rarely said of Menotti's work; that Menotti's direction is little short of perfect; that as satire it sometimes misses its target; that as spectacle it is one of the most sumptuous staged by La Fenice in recent years.

May 17: This is Menotti's last day in Venice, crowded with packing, last-minute advice to the cast, entertaining ten guests at dinner, on the run, en route to La Fenice for the show. Tomorrow he leaves for London, Bath, and Bristol—and *Martin*. Then on to Vienna for two days for the Austrian première of *The Bishop*. And then to Spoleto, three weeks from today, for two months of uninterrupted work on the Festival. A breakneck life.

A breakneck life: once commonplace in the opera business.

A breakneck life: the "prison years" which Verdi resented, which kept Rossini, Donizetti, Giovanni Pergolesi, Jommelli, Johann Hasse, Mayr, Cavalli, and hosts of other composers moving in an unbroken rhythm from composition to performance to composition to performance.

A breakneck life: still the daily lot of opera singers, conductors, impresarios, directors. But no longer, alas, of composers, who are excluded from the present pattern of opera.

Opera is no longer popular, *popolare*, of the people, as it once was in Europe. In North America, of course, it never belonged to the people. It is logical and not surprising that modern opera (specifically *The Medium* and *The Consul*) were able to achieve long runs only when they got *out* of the opera house, onto Broadway, where they were produced for the people by a show producer. There is a bitter lesson here for those who believe that temples of art will automatically mean more work for more composers.

No matter what his critics say, Menotti has reshaped the opera world. He, a composer, working at a time when operatic composition is all but dead, has remade the image of opera and pointed a new way for it. "The long runs of *Medium* and

Consul on Broadway, eight months in all, brought me a regular income and set me free," Menotti says. "They were a turning point for modern opera."

It was Cocteau who praised *The Medium* as a work which "elevates the ordinary and the everyday into lyric drama," and Menotti as a composer whose every opera was a tour de force, "but realized with such grace that any difficulty of execution is concealed." In Menotti's *Medium,* Cocteau conceded, a "new element exists: new, yet as old as the world." That element is humankind. Menotti says of his own works: "I've always conceived my own theatrical works as mirrors of the condition of man *sub specie aeternitatis.*"

Menotti recognizes his importance in the sphere of contemporary opera. "Let's be frank. The success of *The Medium* was a turning point of sorts. Other composers began then to be interested in the commercial possibilities of opera; they began to consider long runs on Broadway, to think about TV opera." Menotti still believes that the long run on or off Broadway is the only salvation for contemporary opera. "Otherwise we have only premières and the work dies quickly. In a long run, you get a new audience every night, and more and more people get to know your work."

Despite the fact many writers regard Menotti as the spark which set fire to the postwar opera renaissance, Menotti himself denies that he is responsible for the revival. Undoubtedly his direction and his humanism are two major factors in the present success of opera, most especially in the United States, but also in Europe and in the Far East. Yet other elements have played a part in opera's recent *reprise.*

While workshops and small opera companies in America, and subsidized groups abroad, were pushing the modern opera wagon with new productions, composers received an additional, unexpected boost from the recording boom—which coincided almost exactly with the opera frenzy. Since the first years of Caruso's success on records, there has never been anything in the history of the phonograph to compare with the postwar interest in recorded music.

The first recorded full-length opera after the war was *La*

Forza del Destino on Cetra, which became an international best seller almost overnight. Implemented by Dario Soria's "Festival of Opera" program broadcast from WOR in New York City, opera records began to roll. RAI (Radio Italiana) and other national networks such as the Canadian Broadcasting Corporation, French Radiodiffusion, the Westdeutsch Rundfunk, Radio Prague, suddenly found that there was a large unexploited market for full-length operas. These programs have become more and more ambitious. RAI now presents opera not only on records, but also commissions works and buys the radio and television rights to new productions from all the various Italian theaters, so that a repertory of nearly one hundred operas is heard each year in addition to those thirty-odd works seen on RAI-TV. In German-speaking countries, an even larger plan has been put into effect, using live operas, recordings, and tapes.

It was inevitable that composers, no less than singers, should benefit from this, though probably no composer owes recordings as large a debt as do, for example, Maria Callas, Tagliavini, Stignani, Schwarzkopf, or Simionato, whose international reputations were "made" before they had ever sung a note in the United States.

The early Verdi operas, *Rosenkavalier, Wozzeck, La Sonnambula, I Puritani,* even *Les Dialogues des Carmélites* enjoy a larger and more knowledgeable public because they were already familiar through records before being widely played onstage in America. Moreover, records have raised the level of taste in this country and made experts of us all, thus inflicting one kind of hardship on the small professional opera company. The hardship arises primarily because a recording is made from a perfect, or near-perfect tape. This tape is fabricated from more than two thousand little bits and pieces of tape, so that a singer can sing ten bad notes and still have a perfect tone come out on the finished recording. All the roughness and the errors have been eliminated by sound engineers, so that the man who buys an opera recording in a supermarket or music house takes home a synthetic product, not a live show. He is therefore often gravely disappointed when he hears the "real thing," most especially on the professional level, for few people expect college or workshop productions to sound like big-scale opera company offerings. Whether or not recordings have eaten into the paying, theater-going public is a moot point.

Recordings have certainly spread the opera gospel around the world. This much cannot be denied. Nor has the saturation point yet been reached. The markets of Europe are still buying at full speed, while those of Japan, Turkey, Israel, Greece, and the African countries have just begun to open up. The phenomenon particular to the United States fifteen to twenty years ago has just begun to reach these areas, where opera is only now taking hold. In all these areas, the recording industry can widen the public for any opera, old or new, if it will.

The possible benefits to the composer cannot be overestimated, for the singer always has his public, while the composer must now seek his public out. The most serious obstacle is the hostility of the public toward modern music. "What can we do?" asks the director of one of Italy's biggest opera houses, with a shrug. "The public won't buy it. When we schedule a new work, the house is empty. They don't want it." This is a dilemma which recording companies could help solve, by trying to shape public taste. Eventually they must decide whether it is truly right to make yet another *Aida* or *Traviata* or *Carmen* —the tenth or the twentieth complete recording of one of these works—or to make that first *Susannah* or *Intolleranza 1960* or *Night Flight* or *Die Kluge*. They will have to choose a course— whether like the opera houses they will continue to be museums preserving hallowed relics, which they dust off occasionally, or whether they will become something aesthetically and intellectually meaningful.

The composers of modern music face special problems in the opera world. Indeed, it is doubtful whether even with the crutches of subsidy and airing on records and television they will be successful. For the public cannot comprehend what Ortega y Gasset calls "dehumanized art." Like abstract expressionists, who paint for themselves, many modern composers appear to write for themselves. This new art is not "accessible to every man," says Ortega, "because its impulses are not of a generically human kind." During the nineteenth century, artists on all levels dealt with human realities. Ortega sees reflected here the democratization of society during that era. It was "normal" to be realistic. Beethoven was realistic and so was Wagner, whose art is of a historical realism, in spite of dragons and magic fire. Verdi, Rossini, Donizetti, Puccini, every one wrote relevant, accessible works, operas which could be understood by the ruling monarch or the peasant. Contemporary art, on the other hand, divides the public into two classes: those who understand and those who do not. The "ins" and the "outgroup." It is an artist's art, not for general consumption. Thus the public has been lost.

At the box office of an opera house, modern works are nearly all poison. Dehumanized, they avoid living reality. While in the nineteenth century, artists lent humanity a certain dignity and mobility, the modern composer often takes an almost perverse delight in stripping away these very qualities and assaulting the ear with cacophony.

No one denies that Lukas Foss's *Time-Cycle* is art. "Anything can be art," says Ezra Pound. Box-office figures prove that the public will not pay to hear a program made up exclusively of such music. An evening of opera is not like a concert, where the program includes one Beethoven and one Brahms and one fifteen-minute modern piece. An evening of opera is all modern or, where modern music is barely tolerated, not modern at all.

"Dio Santo! What a bore!" cries the Milanese gentleman at the première of a new atonal work. Probably its première will also be its closing performance, or it may survive for two or three nights before it dies, even though La Scala sometimes tries to mitigate the pain by running modern operas on double bills with familiar works. But still the public stays away. Listeners cannot understand anything they hear, they cannot identify with the drama, they cannot recognize anything familiar save the human shapes moving around in costume onstage. Because they are not invited to participate—or is it because they are not being entertained?—they reject modern opera. Only certain very special audiences such as Trieste, Venice, the New York City Opera, **Santa Fe, and** certain German and

Slavic countries tolerate novelties; elsewhere they are likely to be greeted with hoots or shouts of *"Assez!"* or *"Basta!"* or, as in the case of a modern work given recently in Italy, with unbroken, gelid silence.

At times the university audience may welcome an *avant-garde* composition, a subsidized audience listening to subsidized music; but the paying opera public will not. Without the generous support of the Ford Foundation, one fears that the New York City Opera's seasons of modern American opera would collapse. And how many of these heavily subsidized works have entered the repertory? It will be a miracle if the Metropolitan Opera's National Company can impose *Susannah* on the public, when *Wozzeck* and *Rake's Progress* and *Peter Grimes* and *Murder in the Cathedral* and several hundred other worthy works are still outside the magic circle. Not that these operas have no merit, but that the public has no taste for them. If a work has not become part of the regular musical tradition of a country in a decade, or twenty years, when may it hope to succeed?

Comparing Menotti's and Britten's success with the failures of their contemporaries, one cannot help concluding that they have a public because they have, as Menotti says, "reached out a hand" to bridge the gap. Humanism enters the picture here as the force opposing "dehumanized art." In order to get a hearing, other composers may be compelled to subscribe to humanism, just as, in another field, the literary *avant-garde* now shows signs of having modified its extreme position to please public taste. Ortega's "young artist," be he sculptor, painter, or composer, needs acceptance if he is to survive.

In this context it is valuable to consider what Henry Pleasants says in his difficult and controversial book *The Agony of Modern Music:*

> "The serious composer has lost touch with the currents of popular taste . . . It is his failure to meet contemporary requirements that distinguishes the contemporary composer from composers of any earlier epoch. Previously it could always be said that composers represented the taste and emotional and intellectual characteristics of their own time . . . Then there was a

demand for composers. There was a demand for their music, and they could make a living from accommodating the demand. Now the festivals of contemporary music, the grants, fellowships and commissions to contemporary composers must be interpreted as . . . evidence of decrepitude, not of vitality. If modern music had any real vitality, it would take its place normally within the framework of contemporary musical life and make its own way."

Further, from Honegger:

"The collapse of music is obvious . . . Nor is anything to be gained from resisting it . . . The profession of composer discloses the singularity . . . of a person who troubles himself to produce something for which there are no consumers."

When we reach an uncompromising composer such as Arnold Schönberg's son-in-law Luigi Nono, we have an artist who holds to its own musical concepts and tries to draw the public at another level—as a participant in the opera. Talking of the need for a "new musical theater," Nono lashes out at the "dernier-cri, Dior mentality" critics and puts forth his own revolutionary ideas. No longer, he says, can we have a three-step process: first, the libretto; then the music; then, at last, the stage direction, "as a structure made up of prefabricated parts which are put together piece by piece to make the whole." Nono urges a direct and simultaneous process, the theater of ideas, of situations, of conscience, in which the public "is not limited to passive attendance at a rite."

Nono's idea of production, in fact, is not far removed from that of Roberto Rossellini or Federico Fellini and others who work without a script, filming from "ideas" alone. He would throw public and performers together, abandoning the traditional separation of the two. Regarding Schönberg's *Die glückliche Hand*, a "drama with music" presented in 1924 in Vienna and in 1954 in Cologne, as the take-off point for modern musical theater; and being the husband of Schönberg's daughter, Nono has a direct family tie with the German master which may make him the bridge between the "death" of opera in the twenties and the "rebirth" which may soon come.

He sees in such works as Berg's *Lulù* and Dallapiccola's *The Prisoner* the beginnings of an operatic "theater of situations," steps toward a truly modern opera, which he already sees—for idea, at least—in the Brecht-Weill *Rise and Fall of the City of Mahagonny* (full length version) and in Hindemith.

Nono's own opera *Intolleranza 1960* caused an uproar at La Fenice when it was first given there, but the disturbances were more political than musical. Widely performed in Eastern Europe, the opera had its first exposure in the United States in the Boston Opera Group's production in 1965.

Intolleranza, a formal music drama which must be rehearsed and cannot unfold according to invention *in situ,* has a cast and a conductor; the public plays no part in it. In this, at least, it is conventional and does not conform to Nono's new formulas. But quite probably this conventionality gives it a better chance to enter the repertory than the improvised works which Nono now favors. In these, certain "contact points" are fixed in advance, but everything else is left to the fantasy of the director, the musicians, even the scenic painter who may work onstage as the work progresses. The only factors established in advance are the moment when the work would begin (one cannot say "When the curtain would go up," for the curtain would be abandoned as an undesirable barrier between the reality onstage and the reality offstage) and the length of time each of the various components would hold the stage—rather like a debate. Nono admits that this kind of theater would be "essentially a trial," yet he thinks of it as a step toward something else, a new theater which would have permanent form. Yet Nono's theory of opera is not as radical as it seems at first glance.

His "collective theater" may lead the art of opera along a new path, although even Menotti, whom Nono regards as hopelessly reactionary, began long ago to write his libretto and compose his music simultaneously, plotting the direction as he works rather than thinking of each function as a separate unit. The idea of joining audience and performers, too, has been tried out in many countries, although it has not been used often in opera.

As for Nono's scheme for having the public flow freely in and out of the theater, listen to and watch what it wishes, chat with friends during the "performance," participate, sit or stand as it likes, such a public already exists—but not in the theater. It is the congregation of the churches of the Latin world, who act as if the nave were the living room of a community dwelling.

Once it reaches this point, opera will have come full circle. Recent studies made in the various archives of Venice suggest that opera as we know it dates not from the Renaissance but from Venetian secular and sacred dramas of the Middle Ages. From there, it is only a leap back to Marco Polo's Hangchow and the temple and teahouse theaters, where a form of opera, the Chinese music drama, has been exposed to the public for nearly two thousand years.

Let us ask ourselves whether opera has not finally returned to the house of its origins. From Chinese temples; from the church altars of the Veneto; from the democratic theaters of sixteenth-century Venice to the university theaters of the United States; from Florentine or Roman *palazzi* to the new temples of art, the opera houses of the world, and to those modern churches where opera is regularly performed—there has been a natural progression accomplished not in three and a half centuries, as pedants would have it, but in five hundred, a thousand, or two thousand years. At each point in its rich history, opera has existed because the composer gave it life, because he imposed upon it the spiritual and cultural values of his time, because he served as prophet and seer in the creative act.

CHAPTER

X

OPERA TOMORROW:
BOOM OR BUST

To predict a long-term future in general terms for opera is impossible, for opera is not one world, but four: first, the United States, including Hawaii; second, Western Europe, England, South and Central America; third, the German-speaking and Slavic countries; and last, China. Each of these geographic regions has its own special operatic character, its own peculiar operatic problems. In each area, ultimate success or failure is possible; the operatic pattern is everywhere different, though certain basic similarities exist.

On all four operatic "continents" some form of music drama is staged as a serious art, although the repertories vary. Russia, China, and the Slavic and German countries all support classical and modern national works which are rarely or never heard outside the country of their origin. Hindemith's *Mathis der Maler*, Hans Erich Pfitzner's *Palestrina*, Leoš Janáček's *Jenufa* and *Katya Kabanova* are good examples of the type. The other regions of the opera world share the same general repertory, which is called the "standard repertory," with local preferences accounting for variations within that frame: *Don Carlo*'s popularity in New York, for example, or *Faust*'s in Paris.

Singers, too, must choose between an eastern and a western world. There is a free exchange of artists between Europe and the Americas, Japan and Australia and New Zealand; in all these areas, local talent is supplemented by imported stars. But only a few singers cross the Iron Curtain, while China is completely independent of the operatic world-trade circle. Not even the recent spurt of interest in western music in China has caused a breach in that wall. China neither lends nor borrows talent.

In all four sectors of the opera world, the art is now healthy, although it often seems most firmly established in Germany, the Slavic countries and China, where it seems ineradicable. In Italy, France, and Great Britain, crises and threats of closure are too often heard; yet one suspects that these cries are raised only to force additional government subsidy. There has been a distinct pickup in audience interest in Western Europe since 1950. Tickets in the highest price brackets are often the most difficult to obtain. Artists' fees continue to soar. Few people now speak of opera as a bore. In short: signs of continuing prosperity, accompanied by rising prices on both sides of the Iron Curtain.

In the United States, opera lives two lives: one on the professional stage, the other in the cotton-padded, shielded netherworld of the university workshop. And in this country, sad to say, the future of professional opera, save that in the biggest cities, is by no means assured in spite of the current vogue of art centers and culture temples. It is too early to predict success or failure for the national traveling companies of the Metropolitan; these now serve cities which have no permanent companies of their own. But if these traveling groups were to fail, a serious breach in the opera world would result. No fears need be expressed for the workshops, unique in the world. They will flourish, their future assured, predicated upon increasing enrollments in colleges, universities, and conservatories which are subsidized by state, federal, and private funds.

The 227 workshops which are functioning in 1964-65 will undoubtedly maintain their present high standards in choice of repertory, and will also continue at their present high technical level. This, because they can choose operas without considering box-office figures and because they have more time for rehearsal than professional companies. Unless the tradition of more-technique-than-feeling changes, however, workshop opera will in the future be marred by that certain flatness, that sterility and whiteness which too often flaw its productions. Perhaps it is too much to hope that a college-age performer will interpret, will cast off embarrassment and throw himself wholly into his part. No one expects a drama department *Lear* to sound like an Old Vic production. Yet the primacy of technique over spirit, of mechanics over heart, has long been a central problem in American university-level music enterprises. Workshop opera is naturally afflicted. The future problem of the workshop is not whether it shall survive, but whether it can improve, can rise above pedantry; whether mere neatness of production will be considered sufficient recompense for the subsidies made available through music department and opera department budgets. Still more perplexing is the problem of whether it is wise to train thousands of young professionals for a profession which has no use for them. This raises certain questions of utility and relevance which are too intricate, if not too painful, to be dealt with here. These problems notwithstanding, the workshop seems to be here to stay, at least as long as the university boom lasts.

Professional companies in the United States are on less solid ground, for they face rising production costs at a time when few great artists are available, when far too many productions barely rise above amateur level, when the public is showing increasing preoccupation with creeping inflation, when our military entanglements abroad are cutting into the pleasure-will of the people. The Metropolitan and San Francisco opera companies are assured of survival; but some of the smaller civic enterprises may find the future bleak, even with the encouraging support they now receive from the Ford Foundation. Some twenty of these companies have died in the last two decades, perhaps because of the absorption of first- and second-generation Italians into a predominantly Anglo-Saxon culture, perhaps because this kind of opera can no longer meet the competition of touring units sent out from New York, Boston, or San Francisco. Another factor in their failure has been the difficulty of raising funds for opera in small cities: in the large urban centers, foundation and corporation aid are available to supplement private contributions.

As the small civic enterprise atrophies, big opera is growing bigger. The Metropolitan now has a season of more than thirty weeks, for the first time in its history; Chicago's single *Don Giovanni* has grown into a full fall season. San Francisco now boasts a cadet company and a spring season. Each of these companies should continue to grow, either through extension of the season or through addition of infant companies under the parent wing.

Metropolitan art centers, being built to house the performing arts, raise specters of their own, especially for opera. Not the least of these is the suspicion that these palaces are being built for a cultural elite, not for the people. While an old, run-down theater on a back street may have something homely and inviting about it, the glittering pile set apart in a garden of concrete walkways, decorative planting, and abstract sculpture is likely to discourage any but the most cold-blooded adventurer. So much has been written about the unsuitability of these arts centers as homes for the arts that it seems unnecessary to expand on the subject here. Yet one cannot help feeling that an architectural setting which is hostile to art can only aggravate the already troublesome problem of attracting the public. The dehumanization of the urban center is discouraging enough; add to it the dehumanization of architecture, and the little man with the ticket in his hand feels out of place before he reaches his seat. The terrible experience of the Metropolitan Opera with the New Theatre (1909-10) makes one fearful that other such fiascos may be in the making. Cities investing in multimillion-dollar art centers ought to take the New Theatre lesson to heart: a pile of bricks and mortar does not make a theater. Art cannot be created with money. A second lesson: the theatergoer ought to feel as comfortable in the theater as in his own house. The problem is one of atmosphere as well as size.

It is this sense of belonging which is necessary above all else. Here we are thrust at once to the center of a problem which has involved generations of American operagoers: the basic mistrust which an Anglo-Saxon puritanical people feel toward a too-opulent art which often gives too much pleasure. Even England cannot be compared to the United States in this area, for there the Cavaliers once ruled. The English theater tradition is far stronger than ours, though it seems puny compared to Latin, Greek, or Chinese enterprises. Peculiarly American is the fear of the theater. One does not wonder that opera and drama have had to take refuge in the university, there to be nursed by pedants. So long as art is a part of school curriculum, it can be tolerated as something useful, instructive. The puritan ethic can permit this, although it cannot tolerate the love of art for pure aesthetic or sensual pleasure. This is a purely American problem. Perhaps we shall not have a living theater until we breed more hedonists.

The molding of public taste is of equal importance to the housing and nourishing of opera itself, for democracy has, at best, been unkind to art. In the United States opera especially is not an integrated part of the culture as it is in Europe, South America, or China. Our government has not dignified opera in the past by subsidy. Radio and television networks ignore it. If the Texas Company had not brought the country twenty-six years of Saturday matinees, the score would be near zero.

In European countries, as in Canada, where radio and television are not operated solely upon the profit motive, the arts are regularly included in programing. In the last six months of 1965, for example, the Italian national television network gave full-length, staged, costumed televised performances of twelve operas: *Il Cordovano, Il Diavolo Zoppo, Don Pasquale, I Due Baroni di Roccazzurra, Carmen, Tosca, Il Barbiere di Siviglia, L'Elisir d'Amore, La Figlia del Reggimento, Andrea Chénier, Martin's Lie,* and *Canto di Natale.* Ten recitals by such artists as Simionato, Cesare Siepi, and Sutherland were also programed.

During the same period, Americans had to be content with a taped *Amahl* and a single Sunday-night glimpse of Joan Sutherland's Violetta, accommodated between jugglers and borscht-circuit comedians. Opera, like concert music, simply does not get enough exposure on the national communications media. All Americans who lie outside the range of the Canadian Broadcasting Corporation transmissions are culturally deprived.

On a typical autumn weekend there were thirty-six hours of football programed on Saturday afternoon and thirty-seven hours of football on Sunday afternoon. Seventy-three hours of football in two six-hour listening periods on ten channels. Against this, *thirty minutes* of the Grand Rapids Symphony was programed, a ratio of 146 to 1. In the entire fall, during which the Metropolitan, San Francisco, and Chicago season's were in full swing, not one single act of opera was broadcast from their stages on a national network.

The bald truth is that the United States, a secular nation dedicated to the production of goods, has no real operatic heritage, either at the top or at the bottom of its society. Neither its repertory nor its audience is thoroughly representative: we have no masterworks based on national myth, no *Boris*, no *Meistersinger*, no *Nabucco*. Nor have we a public which cuts through all social and economic levels. The chief components of the American opera audience are the educated upper and upper-middle classes, and few enough even of those. General Electric and Ford run no chartered buses to the Met and San Francisco, as Fiat and Olivetti do to La Scala. We have no equivalent for that unparalleled "center of culture," the *dopolavoro* or afterwork club where stevedores, truckers, crane operators, and gondoliers gather to shoot pool, play cards, eat and drink, play the jukebox and sing. Opera plays a major role in the afterwork club repertory, as it does in late-night Italian restaurants. In France, Germany, Canada, and other nations operatic music is played with sufficient frequency on radio and television to make it familiar to anyone who turns the dials.

Not being integrated into American life at any level, can opera continue to flourish in this country at the pitch it has maintained over the last ten years? Will the opera business profit from Presidential decrees, publicity, and arts bills, thus sharing in the great pie-in-the-sky which is the culture boom? The best one can hope for is slow victory, founded on the progress made since World War II. European opera has already passed through its crisis and is on the way to recovery. For America, the crisis may still lie ahead. For a national run on art does not by any means guarantee a national run on opera. High-brow titles now appear with consoling regularity on the lists of Book-of-the-Month Club and Literary Guild. Film makers offer Tennessee Williams, Edward Albee, and other superior dramatists as regular Saturday night fare. Van Gogh sells in the five-and-ten, while Mondrian canvases are adapted into dress fabrics. The grade-school teacher may take her students to a museum; she is far less likely to take them to a performance. Opera has just begun to filter down from the top. It still remains enthroned in splendid isolation way up there, among the educated, far above the mob. But this is wrong, of course.

What the United States needs, apparently, is not more temples of Capital-A-Art, but more absorption at ground level. Acrobats and comedians cannot soil *Traviata:* opera has been popular entertainment in the past. In many countries of the world it is popular today. And *Traviata* can use all the exposure it can get on the mass media. Here America is the pauper of the world. As long as classical music remains segregated on FM (and even there one hears little enough of it), as long as it is enclosed in dust-proof sanctuaries, it will remain extraneous to life in this country. When it is accepted by those who cater to the public, then the public will accept it. This problem is central to any broadening of the opera public in the United States. For all the forward strides made by professional and workshop companies cannot offset, ultimately, the lack of popular understanding and appreciation.

A new price policy is also indicated. The other three operatic "continents" have no price problems, because their opera belongs more completely to the people. There are high-priced tickets, but cheap tickets are also available. In Italy, for example, a ticket to the top balcony costs around three hundred lire, the equivalent of fifty American cents, the price of six Italian newspapers, of seven eggs, of two pounds of bread, of four children's ice-cream bars, of one hour of domestic help, of a cotton handkerchief. The other countries of Western Europe also offer inexpensive tickets, while in Eastern Europe opera is even cheaper. China claims that every citizen of the People's Republic can get into the opera theaters of Peking and Shanghai. In America, on the other hand, opera is priced out of the reach of almost everyone. The cheapest ticket offered by the Chicago Lyric is five dollars: all but the rich are effectively excluded here. In smaller cities, a three dollar bottom is common for opera. (Say nothing of the twenty dollars recently charged by a civic company for orchestra seats for Arrigo Boito's *Mefistofele*.) In far too many theaters the only tickets sold are priced at five and eight dollars.

Compared with European scales, these American prices are the equivalent of thirty newspapers (as against six in Italy), of sixty eggs (as against seven), of twelve pounds of bread (instead of two), of thirty ice-cream bars (against four), of three hours of domestic help, of six cotton handkerchiefs. If American opera tickets were priced at European scale, there would be a bottom price of fifty cents to one dollar, corresponding to over-all film admission prices on both continents. These are the prices which ought to prevail. In China, even a beggar can gain admission to the opera. The theater is a refuge, which is what it ought to be.

It is highly significant that the two oldest American opera companies are the Metropolitan and the Cincinnati Summer Opera, both of which have kept a low admission fee. For decades the Cincinnati company offered entrances for twenty-five and fifty cents. It has survived for forty-odd years; by American operatic attrition rates, it is a veritable dinosaur. The company boasts as well the broadest-based public in the country, having preserved intact its tradition that even those who could not afford a seat could stand, see, and hear without paying. Here opera has been truly popular, as it is in Germany, Austria, the Slavic countries, and in Italy. It is Cincinnati's second most venerable cultural institution.

If other companies are to achieve comparable longevity, they must mold their price policy along similar lines, remembering that for every man who earns two hundred dollars a week, there are dozens who earn ninety. Unless the latter also

can hear opera—first through the mass media, then in the
theater—opera will never be truly popular in the United States.
And without popularity, it may survive in this country only as
a diversion for the rich and educated. This would be a grim
fate for a form of entertainment which for centuries had an
audience as lively as a circus public.

Contrast our own situation with that of China, where the
Great World Theater offers a national drama unit, a circus, and
the opera performance from eleven in the morning until eleven
at night, at prices so modest that even the poor are not excluded. There, evidently, there is no gulf between art and the
people.

The question of relevance now comes into play. One of the
most healthful signs of recent times is the composer's concern
for such significant plays as Arthur Miller's *A View from the
Bridge* and T. S. Eliot's *Murder in the Cathedral*. A future for
opera must remain problematical so long as only relics from a
glorious past are staged. Students now think of Ernest Hemingway and William Faulkner as hopelessly passé. They look to
Edward Albee, Norman Mailer, William Burroughs, James
Baldwin and LeRoi Jones as the voice of their age. Opera owes
them at least as much as drama, art, and the novel are giving.

No single factor can be considered more important than
relevance. The success of *The Consul* was no accident: that
opera seized the contemporary public, just as *Le nozze di
Figaro* or *Nabucco* called out a message to the audiences of
their own times. We cannot afford to ignore the implications
of the *Amahl* statistics: nearly five thousand performances in
thirteen years. When opera says what the public wants to hear,
it will be listened to, paid for.

The success of films, from *The Great Train Robbery* and
Birth of a Nation through *The Jazz Singer, The Pawnbroker,*
and *Modesty Blaise,* lies in their appeal not to a chosen elite
but to masses of people. Their creators knew how to capture
the audience, entertain, *intrattenere,* as Cimarosa, Donizetti,
Jommelli, Cavalli, Verdi, and Puccini did, and as Menotti does
—and as exponents of modern music apparently do not. Anyone
who wishes a continued life for opera must hope that it will

again become the "most wanted art" because of its relevance. At present, films, folk music, and drama have seized the public imagination which, not long ago, the people gave freely to opera, without coercion from the upper classes, or from governments, without the pressure of snob appeal.

Opera's purveyors must realize that busy-work does not equal art, that giantism cannot guarantee quality. Even as we live the evening before the long-awaited American cultural explosion, an admonitory voice whispers a few home truths about opera: art centers do not automatically spawn art; centralization and proliferating bureaucracy can strangle both honest and creative impulse; subsidy often encourages mediocrity, indeed, is often necessary because mediocrity cannot earn its own way; art endowments are no panacea for the deep-seated ills of the American opera world. We must beware of the statistics which may reflect private, corporate, and foundation giving, but may not be used as an index of true worth. Beware, most of all, of complacency and self-congratulation, for at the moment opera in this country is passing through a dangerous and critical period. It is characteristically American to think that big numbers (1300 symphony orchestras, 732 opera companies) mean that music is prospering. Actually, as the Rockefeller Brothers' Foundation Report on the Performing Arts points out, most of this activity is at amateur or workshop level. Only fifty-four of those orchestras provide their members with full-time professional employment. Six hundred young American singers are trying to make their way in Europe because they cannot find jobs in the opera business at home. We assuredly have no laurels to rest on.

It is also typically American to believe that an inpouring of dollars and man-hours will cure every ailment. This is not the case with opera. It is our national problem, national challenge, national necessity to educate public taste. Until this first infant's step is taken, no giant strides can be made. Every dial, every index, points to a golden future for the arts in America. But opera will not share the treasure unless we apply to its preparation and production both common sense and wisdom.

NOTES AND ACKNOWLEDGMENTS

1. *On theaters, workshops, and audiences: Enciclopedia dello Spettacolo,* articles on *compagnia* and on many of the specific companies analyzed; *Opera News,* both the magazine itself and the running file which it has kept on opera for twenty-five years. Much information was provided by individual companies; and I am especially grateful to Messrs. Rudolf Bing, John Gutman, Francis Robinson, and Robert Herman of the Metropolitan; Messrs. Kurt Adler and Herbert Scholder and Mrs. Dewey Donnell of San Francisco; Dr. Arturo Di Filippi of Miami; Mr. Julius Rudel of New York City Opera; Mr. Fortune Gallo of San Carlo; the late Oscar Hild, Messrs. Robert Seidell, Fausto Cleva, and Anthony Stivanello of Cincinnati; Miss Carol Fox of Chicago and Mr. Kip Kelley of her Guild Board of Directors; Messrs. Mario Labroca, Franco Ammanati, and G. Pugliese of La Fenice in Venice; Mr. Giuseppe Antonicelli of the Comunale in Trieste; Messrs. Antonio Ghiringhelli and Franco Armani of La Scala; Dr. Lando Ambrosini of RAI; Senator and Mrs. Vincenzo Gagliardi of Venice; Countess Wally Toscanini Castelbarco; Dr. Gaetano Negri of Parma; the Intendants and staffs of Cologne, Zürich, and Mannheim; the Westdeutschrundfunk; Dr. Ludwig Zirner of University of Illinois; Dr. Elemer Nagy of Hartt College in Hartford. Details on Czech theaters were drawn from issues of the English magazine *Opera.* The review of the Hamburg Summer Festival comes from *Le Monde,* August 6, 1964. Robert Herman's remarks on planning the Metropolitan season

are excerpts from a long article published in *Opera News* on March 14, 1964. The report of the International Music Council is also from the August 6, 1964, *Le Monde*. The controversy about demonstrations in the theater can be followed in *Il Gazzettino* of Venice, March 5, 1964, and in the periodical *La Rivista*, published in Parma, in the issues for the spring of 1962; the critical essay on Glyndebourne is from the London *Times*, August 2, 1964. Joseph's Wechsberg's review of Vienna problems and Walter Ducloux' on German provincial opera were written for *Opera News*, as was George Martin's review of Santa Fe Opera.

2. *On management: Enciclopedia dello Spettacolo*, articles on opera, the impresario, the Venetian theater, the Genovese theater, the impresarios Domenico Barbaia and Bartolomeo Merelli; *Opera News*, March 14, 1964; *Opera*, July, 1963.

The information on Covent Garden's employment rolls is drawn from the *Annual Report* of Covent Garden, made available through the courtesy of the British Council in Milan and Mr. Patrick Meade, the British Vice-Consul in Venice. Giuseppina Strepponi's itineraries were compiled by Frank Walker, who published them in his book *The Man Verdi* (Knopf, 1962). The edition of Stendhal used is the Coe translation (Criterion Books); the Benedetto Marcello's *Il Teatro alla Moda* is in the Biblioteca Universale of Rizzoli, Bologna. Information on the Venice and Trieste theaters was made available through the management of those opera houses. The quotation from Mario Labroca comes from a public lecture given at the Ateneo Veneto in the spring of 1964. The vita of Alfredo Salmaggi was provided by the impresario himself and by his sons Mario and Felix. Other sources used are the letters of Verdi, Bellini, and Donizetti, and an unpublished letter of Maria Malibran in the author's collection. The study of Rudolf Bing is from *The New York Times Magazine*, October 11, 1964, written by Martin Mayer and copyrighted by the New York Times company.

3. *On singers: Enciclopedia dello Spettacolo*, Rodolfo Celletti's invaluable article on "the singer"; *Opera and its Future in America*, Herbert Graf. The evaluation of Maria Callas' unique contribution appeared originally in *Le Monde*, while the Di Stefano interview was printed in *Il Tempo*, August 8, 1964. It is reprinted by permission of Aldo Palazzi, Milan, publisher.

I am indebted to the Hon. James Smith of Covent Garden for the Grace Moore anecdote; and to Miss Anita Colombo of Milan, the managements of the Stagione Lirica of the Nuovo in Milan

(A.L.C.I.), the Teatro Lirico Sperimentale in Spoleto, and the Centro di Avviamento in Venice.

My own studies of Malibran and Caffarelli originally appeared in *Opera News* in the "Great Opera Houses" series studies of Venice and Naples.

4. *On composers: Enciclopedia dello Spettacolo;* Dr. Franco Colombo, formerly of G. Ricordi in New York, now head of Franco Colombo, Inc.; *Show* Magazine, which carried Stravinsky's comments on Menotti; *Opera e le Opere,* Guido Pannain (Curci, Milan); *The Dehumanization of Art,* José Ortega y Gasset (New Directions, New York); *New Yorker,* which published Janet Flanner's comments on the *Savage.* I am grateful, too, to Mrs. Dario Soria and to the composers Gian-Carlo Menotti, Ildebrando Pizzetti, Benjamin Britten, Luigi Nono, Luigi Dallapiccola, and to Mrs. Nuria Schönberg Nono and Mr. Ernest De Weerth.

5. *On directors: Enciclopedia dello Spettacolo;* articles on *regista* and on Messrs. Visconti, Wagner, and Zeffirelli; *Wieland Wagner,* Panovsky (Schonemann, Bremen, 1964); *Regia e Registi nel Teatro Moderno,* Vito Pandolfi (Cappelli, Bologna, 1961); *Momenti e Aspetti della Messinscena,* Giuseppe Marchioro (Ricordi, Milan, 1960); *Histoire Illustrée du Théâtre Lyrique,* René Dumesnil (Plon, Paris, 1953).

I wish also to thank Miss Priscilla Morgan; Messrs. Placido Nicolai and Luigi Musci of the Carducci Library in Spoleto; Mrs. Maria Teresa Muraro, Dr. Pietro Nardi, and Dr. Vittorio Branca of the Fondazione Cini in Venice; Miss Lucia Pallavicini of Italian Information Service in New York; Miss Josephine Inzerillo of Italian State Tourist Office, New York; the Internationes Foundation of Bonn; British Information Service, New York and Rome; Mr. Peter Dragadze; the late Carlo Gatti; Mr. John Majeski, former editor and publisher of *Musical America;* Mrs. August Belmont, Mrs. John De-Witt Peltz, Messrs. Frank Merkling and Gerald Fitzgerald of New York; Mr. William Crawford III of New York; the late Mr. Joachim Meyer; Mr. Giorgio D'Andria; Mr. Michael Sweeney of S. Hurok, Inc.; and Mr. Edgar Vincent.

Lastly, I am grateful to Mr. Jesse Carmack of Santa Monica, California, and Mrs. Helen King of New York, whose enthusiasm launched this book and sustained me until it was completed.

INDEX